The Plan for Distance Learning

Marion B. Castellucci

PETERSON'S

THOMSON LEARNING ™

Australia • Canada • Mexico • Singapore • Spain • United Kingdom • United States

PETERSON'S

™

THOMSON LEARNING

About Peterson's

Founded in 1966, Peterson's, a division of Thomson Learning, is the nation's largest and most respected provider of lifelong learning online resources, software, reference guides, and books. The Education Supersite^{SM} at petersons.com—the Web's most heavily traveled education resource—has searchable databases and interactive tools for contacting U.S.-accredited institutions and programs. CollegeQuest® (CollegeQuest.com) offers a complete solution for every step of the college decision-making process. GradAdvantage™ (GradAdvantage.org), developed with Educational Testing Service, is the only electronic admissions service capable of sending official graduate test score reports with a candidate's online application. Peterson's serves more than 55 million education consumers annually.

Thomson Learning is among the world's leading providers of lifelong learning, serving the needs of individuals, learning institutions, and corporations with products and services for both traditional classrooms and for online learning. For more information about the products and services offered by Thomson Learning, please visit www.thomsonlearning.com. Headquartered in Stamford, Connecticut, with offices worldwide, Thomson Learning is part of The Thomson Corporation (www.thomson.com), a leading e-information and solutions company in the business, professional, and education marketplaces. The Corporation's common shares are listed on the Toronto and London stock exchanges.

For more information, contact Peterson's, 2000 Lenox Drive, Lawrenceville, NJ 08648; 800-338-3282; or find us on the World Wide Web at: www.petersons.com/about

ISBN 0-7689-0629-6

Printed in Canada

10 9 8 7 6 5 4 3 2 1   03 02 01

I'd like to thank the many faculty members, administrators, and others who generously shared their knowledge of distance education: Dale Ann Abendroth, Gonzaga University; Michael S. Ameigh, State University of New York at Oswego; Larry Anthony, University of Cincinnati; McRae C. Banks, Worcester Polytechnic Institute; Steven Cammarn, Procter & Gamble; Charles Faulhaber, University of California Berkeley; Irene Kovala, College of DuPage; Fritz J. Messere, State University of New York at Oswego; Karen Novick, Rutgers University; Russell Paden, University of Phoenix Online; Marianne R. Phelps, formerly of the U.S. Department of Education; Mark Pullen, George Mason University; Claudine SchWeber, University of Maryland University College; Steven Shackley, University of California Berkeley; Robert V. Steiner, Columbia University; Kenneth Wachter, University of California Berkeley; and Patti Wolf, University of Maryland University College.

Thanks are also due to the many distance learners who took time out of their busy schedules to explain what distance learning is really like: Cena Barber, Beth Grote, and Randy Ripperger of Drake University; Bardia Khoshnoodi of George Mason University; Robin Barnes, Brigit Dolan, Carla Gentry, Diane Goedde, Patti Iversen, LaVonne Johnson, and Bonnie Schooley of Gonzaga University; Laurie Noe of Nova Southeastern University; Sonja Cole, Diane Krone, Jennifer Lyons, Eva Jeanette Mulvaney, and Richard Shevalier of Rutgers University; Kimberly Foreman of Seton Hall University; Andrea Bessel of State University of New York at Oswego; Scott A. Garrod, Lara Hollenczer, Barbara Rosenbaum, and Kevin Ruthen of Syracuse University; Angela Butcher and Tammy Riegel of the University of Cincinnati; Vania Pogue McBean of University of Maryland University College; Denise Petrosino and Joanne Simon of University of Phoenix Online; Felix Caesar of Walden University; Nicole DeRaleau and Paul Nashawaty of Worcester Polytechnic Institute; and the many other students who wished to remain nameless.

Finally, I'd like to thank Jennifer Rees, Marketing and Communications Coordinator at University of Texas TeleCampus; Karen K. Vignare, Director of Business Development E-Learning at Rochester Institute of Technology; and Robert Ubell, Director of Web-based Distance Learning at Stevens Institute of Technology, for their many valuable suggestions for improving the manuscript.

Marion B. Castellucci

Acknowledgments

Contents

CHAPTER 1: WHAT IS DISTANCE LEARNING?   1

A Brief History of Distance Education   2
Instructional Technologies in Distance Learning   3
What Can You Learn Via Distance Education?   11
Who Offers Distance Learning?   15
How Effective Is Distance Learning?   16
Pursuing Your Education by Distance Learning   18

CHAPTER 2: IS DISTANCE LEARNING RIGHT FOR YOU?   21

The Advantages of Distance Learning   21
The Disadvantages of Distance Learning   23
Assessing Yourself   25
A Mini Self-Assessment   37
Conclusion   40

CHAPTER 3: WHAT CAN YOU STUDY VIA DISTANCE LEARNING?   43

Undergraduate Degree Programs   44
Graduate Degree Programs   49
Certificate Programs   51
Individual Courses   53
Finding Programs and Courses   55

CHAPTER 4: WHO OFFERS DISTANCE EDUCATION?   57

Traditional Colleges and Universities   58
Consortia   59
Comparing the Single University to the Consortium   66
Virtual Universities   67
The New Online Providers   68

CHAPTER 5: SELECTING A GOOD DISTANCE LEARNING PROGRAM   69

Reputation   70
Accreditation   71
Program Quality   76
Advising and Other Services   81
Residency Requirement   82

LC
5805
.C27
2001

Time Frames	82
Cost	83
Your Personal Checklist	83

CHAPTER 6: TAKING STANDARDIZED ADMISSIONS TESTS — 85

Undergraduate Admissions Tests	87
Graduate Admissions Tests	89
Tests of English Language Proficiency	95
Preparing for a Standardized Test	96
Reducing Test Anxiety	97

CHAPTER 7: APPLYING FOR ADMISSION TO DEGREE PROGRAMS — 99

Deadlines	99
Parts of an Application	100
The Application Form	102
Transcripts	103
Letters of Recommendation	103
The Personal Essay	107
Interviews	114
Submitting Your Application	115
In Summary	115

CHAPTER 8: PAYING FOR YOUR EDUCATION — 117

Looking for Low-Cost Alternatives	117
Types of Financial Aid	118
The Language of Financial Aid	119
Federal Financial Aid	121
State Aid Programs	126
Locating Information about Financial Aid	129
Applying for Financial Aid	132
Tax Benefits for Students	135
Paying for School Is Possible	138

CHAPTER 9: SUCCEEDING AS A DISTANCE LEARNER — 141

Mastering the Technology	141
Learning about Library Resources	143

Managing Your Time   145
Managing Time in Online Courses   146
Managing Time in Videotaped Courses   148
Communicating with Faculty   150
Reaching Out to Your Fellow Students   151
Enlisting Your Family's Support   154
In Conclusion   155

APPENDIX   **157**
Resources   157

GLOSSARY   **181**

What Is Distance Learning?

Chapter 1

One student is a busy professional who needs to update work-related skills by taking a couple of computer applications courses in his spare time. Another student, a working mother, never finished her bachelor's degree and would love to have that diploma and get a better job. A third student attends a local community college, but what he'd really like is a degree offered by a four-year institution halfway across the country—without moving. Another would-be student is employed full-time in a field in which a master's degree, perhaps even a doctorate, would really give her career a boost. What all these diverse people have in common is an already full life. For them, disrupting family and work by commuting to sometimes distant on-campus classes on a rigid schedule is simply not a workable option. Instead, students like these are turning to distance learning in order to pursue their educational goals. For many people, and perhaps you, distance learning is a blessing—it means you can get the education you need, which might otherwise be difficult or impossible to obtain in the traditional manner.

What, exactly, is distance learning (also called distance education)? Broadly defined, distance learning is the delivery of educational programs to students who are off site. In a distance learning course, the instructor is not in the same place as the student; the students may be widely separated by geography and time; and the instructor and students communicate with each other using various means, from the U.S. mail to the Internet. Students that take a distance education course are called distance learners, whether they live 300 miles from the university or right across the street.

Distance learning makes use of many technologies, and courses are structured in many different ways. Adding to the variety of distance learning programs provided by traditional institutions of higher education are programs offered by new types of institutions, many worthy, others known as diploma mills, that help to fuel the growth in distance education. With so many technologies, courses, programs, and institutions involved in distance education, your distance learning options can be confusing at first. However, it's critical that you understand what distance education involves and which institutions offer a solid education *before* you enroll. That way you'll be sure that you spend your effort, time, and money wisely on a reputable education.

In this chapter, we'll give you an overview of distance learning; in Chapter 2, we'll help you determine whether or not distance education is right for you; and then in later chapters we'll give you enough background and guidance so you can make an informed choice when selecting a program. We'll also provide suggestions for handling the application process, paying for your education, and making the most of your distance learning experience.

A BRIEF HISTORY OF DISTANCE EDUCATION

In the last five to ten years, distance education has mushroomed, so it's easy to think of it as a completely recent phenomenon. However, today's distance education, based primarily on video and Internet technologies, has its roots in the correspondence courses that arose in the late 1800s. Instructors would send print materials to students by mail, and students would do their assignments and return them by mail. Correspondence courses were asynchronous; that is, the student was not tied to the instructor's timetable. He or she would do the work when it was convenient. Correspondence courses still exist, mostly for single courses, but they have lost ground over the last seventy years to more modern technologies. The first generation of technology that began to supplant correspondence courses was radio in the 1930s, followed by broadcast television in the 1950s and 1960s. Radio and television courses provided one-way communication, and so they were most suitable for delivering information from the faculty to the students. Typically, there was only minimal interaction between instructor and students, and no interaction at all among students. Another constraint on radio and television courses was time. Broadcast courses are synchronous; students had to be listening to the radio or watching television when the course was broadcast, or they would miss the class.

By about 1960, the advent of cable television, audiocassette recorders, and videocassette recorders solved the time problem posed by the earlier broadcast courses. Courses could be broadcast over cable channels several times so students could watch at their convenience. With a VCR or tape recorder, a student could record a lecture or class session when it was broadcast and view or hear it at any time. In fact, recorders made broadcasting unnecessary. The content of a course could be recorded on an audiocassette or videotape and sent to students, who could listen or view it when they had time. Although recording technology provided convenience for students, because courses are asynchronous, it did not solve the major drawback of broadcast courses—the lack of interaction among faculty members and students.

Beginning in the 1980s, the personal computer, two-way audio and videoconferencing, and the Internet greatly expanded the scope of distance education. With these new technologies, much more information could be conveyed from the faculty to students. More important, two-way communication became possible, using interactive video technology or e-mail, newsgroups, bulletin boards, and chat rooms on the Internet. Today, distance education makes use of a wide range of technologies.

In distance learning, courses are *synchronous*, meaning that instructor and students have to meet at a specified time; or they are *asynchronous*, meaning that students can do their work at their own convenience.

INSTRUCTIONAL TECHNOLOGIES IN DISTANCE LEARNING

Today's distance learning courses can be divided into several main categories according to the primary technologies they use to deliver instruction: print-based courses, audio-based courses, video-based courses, and Internet-based courses. The audio, video, and Internet courses all have variations that are synchronous—classes take place at specific times only—and asynchronous—classes that occur at flexible times that may be more convenient for the student.

Print-Based Courses

Correspondence courses use print materials as the medium of instruction. Students receive the materials by mail at the start of the course and return completed assignments by mail. Sometimes fax machines are used to speed up the delivery of assignments, and the telephone can be used if communication between instructor and student is necessary. Patti Iversen, who lives in Montana, completed part of her Bachelor of Science in Nursing degree from the University of Mary in North Dakota by correspondence course. "The correspondence courses offered no direct contact with the instructor or other students," she recalls. "I purchased a syllabus and book and was otherwise on my own." In addition to the lack of interaction between instructor and students, correspondence courses have the disadvantage of being slow. The low-tech nature of a print-based course means lots of delay between assignments and feedback. Of course, the low-tech nature of the course is an advantage, too. Students don't have to invest in expensive technology and can do their work anywhere. Even though print materials continue to play a very important role in distance learning, they are now usually supplemented by more modern instructional technologies.

Audio-Based Courses

Audio-based courses may involve two-way communication, as in audio or phone conferencing; or they may involve one-way communication, including radio broadcast and prerecorded audiotapes sent to students. Fritz J. Messere, associate professor and coordinator of broadcasting at the State University of New York at Oswego, recalls the first time, in 1981, he was involved in teaching a course that used phone conferencing. Once a week, faculty members and students from ten universities as well as representatives from the Federal Communications Commission "met" for a class. "The first three weeks were chaotic," recalls Messere. "We didn't know who was talking." However, they worked out a plan in which a different faculty member moderated the session each week by asking questions. At midsession there was a break, followed by a round-robin discussion, in which each site participated in a predetermined sequence.

According to the National Center for Education Statistics of the U.S. Department of Education, audio-based technologies are not widely used today, with only about 12 percent of institutions of higher learning reporting their use as the primary means of delivering a course in 1997–1998. Instead, audio technologies may be used to supplement the main technology used in the course. For example, in an Internet-based distance education course, students and professors may call one another periodically.

Video-Based Courses

Video-based technologies include two-way interactive video conferencing, one-way video with two-way audio, one-way live video, and one-way prerecorded videotapes provided to students. Of these, two-way interactive video and prerecorded videotapes are the most popular. Of the institutions of higher learning surveyed by the U.S. Department of Education, 54 percent used two-way interactive video and 47 percent used prerecorded videotapes as the primary mode of instructional delivery in their distance education courses.

Two-Way Interactive Video

A course taught by means of two-way interactive video takes place simultaneously in two or more sites. The instructor is located in the home site with a group of students, and other students are located in satellite sites, often with a facilitator to help out. Each site has TV monitors or large screens on which the instructor and students can be viewed. One student in a biology of horticulture course at the University of Cincinnati described the technology used in her course: "Both [home and satellite] classrooms are set up with cameras and two video screens each, which show what is going on in both classrooms. There is a technical assistant present in each location, one on the main campus to set things up and work with the camera, etc., and another in the remote location to set equipment up and to adjust settings should there be any problems." The course itself was conducted as a lecture: "For the most part, the instructor lectures, with students occasionally asking or answering questions. When any student speaks in class, they press a button on a little apparatus on the desk in front of them, which makes the camera point to them as they speak and allows their voice to be

"Both [home and satellite] classrooms are set up with cameras and two video screens each, which show what is going on in both classrooms," reports a student in a course taught by two-way interactive video.

transmitted to the other location." Quizzes and exams are faxed to the satellite site and faxed back or mailed by an assistant when they are completed. Like the best classroom teaching, two-way interactive video works well when the instructor is comfortable with "performing" on camera. "You have to keep students at all sites involved with you by making the lecture as entertaining as possible," says Dr. Larry Anthony, coordinator of the addiction studies baccalaureate program based at the University of Cincinnati. "I've had to adapt my teaching to the medium. For example, instead of using overheads as I might in a regular classroom, I'm more inclined to use a series of PowerPoint slides because they're more entertaining."

Two-way interactive video bridges geographical distances but not time. Students must be in a particular place at a particular time to take the course.

Prerecorded Video

A far less sophisticated, though almost as popular, means of instruction is prerecorded videotape. Each course session is videotaped and mailed to off-site students. To supplement this, the course may have a Web site where notes and assignments are posted, or these may be mailed to the off-site students along with the tapes. If students have any questions, they can call or e-mail the instructor after they view the tape. For many students, the lack of interactivity is made up for by the benefit of "attending" class at their own convenience. Nicole DeRaleau, who is studying for a Master of Engineering degree at Worcester Polytechnic Institute in Massachusetts, says, "Watching the videotaped class is really not very different from sitting in class, except that I can't raise my hand and ask questions." On the other hand, she points out that the asynchronous nature of prerecorded video is an advantage: "I can watch half a class at one sitting, and the other half at a later time. I often work late, and I don't have to worry about missing class."

Internet-Based Courses

Today many distance learning courses, called online courses or e-learning, are offered over the Internet. In 1997–1998, almost 80 percent of the institutions of higher education surveyed by the National

> **"Watching the videotaped class is really not very different from sitting in class, except that I can't raise my hand and ask questions,"** comments distance learner Nicole DeRaleau.

Center for Education Statistics used the Internet as the primary technology in some of their distance education courses. Some online courses use synchronous, "real-time" instruction based primarily on interactive computer conferencing or chat rooms. However, most Internet-based courses use asynchronous instruction, making use of online course management systems, Web sites, e-mail, electronic mailing lists, newsgroups, bulletin boards, and messaging programs.

In asynchronous online courses, instructors post instructional material and assignments, including text, images, video, audio, and even interactive simulations, on the course Web site. Using messaging systems, newsgroups, or bulletin boards, they can start online discussions by posting a comment or question; students can log on using a password and join the discussion at their convenience. In some courses there may be periodic "real-time" interaction in chat rooms or interactive environments like MUDS (multiple-user dungeons) and MOOs (multiple-object orientations). Feedback and guidance to individual students can be done by e-mail or telephone. Note that most of the interaction in an online course is text-based; instructors and students communicate primarily through the keyboarded word. Joanne Simon, who is earning a Master of Business Administration degree from the University of Phoenix Online, describes the setup of her courses: "We use newsgroup folders—the main classroom, a chat room, a course material folder, an assignment folder, and four study group folders. We post a minimum of three messages per day to the main folder in which that week's readings are discussed. In those messages we encourage other students to share ideas, experiences, and opinions on various topics . . . ." Besides this seminar-style interaction, there are many assignments, according to Simon. "We also submit weekly summaries, one graded group assignment, and two personal assignments weekly." Needless to say, students must have a computer with the appropriate software and Internet access in order to take an Internet-based course. The cost of technology aside, online distance learning programs have considerable advantages. Because the course material stays on line for a period of time, students can log on at their own convenience. "There are time stamps on everything they submit," says Michael S. Ameigh,

> **"We use newsgroup folders—the main classroom, a chat room, a course material folder, an assignment folder, and four study group folders,"** explains an online distance learner.

Assistant Provost for Distance Learning and Information Resources and Associate Professor of Communication Studies at the State University of New York at Oswego. "I can see that students are often working in the middle of the night." This flexibility is one of the main attractions of online courses for students, but it can also be its main disadvantage. "It's a common misperception that online courses can be dropped into and out of," says Claudine SchWeber, Assistant Vice President for Distance Education and Lifelong Learning at the University of Maryland University College. Without class sessions to attend at scheduled times, the impetus to log on and do course work must come from within, which requires a great deal of self-discipline.

To help ensure that students keep up, many instructors structure the learning environment by setting weekly deadlines for reading lectures and completing assignments, requiring group projects, and making participation in online discussions mandatory. "I personally contact students who do not participate," says Fritz Messere, who has been teaching broadcasting and business courses online for several years. "Students must interact with me in order to pass the course." At the University of Phoenix Online, students are required to log on to a course and post messages five days out of seven as one of the requirements for passing. In online courses with participation requirements, the amount of interaction between the faculty and students is far greater than in a large lecture class held on campus. There's no lying low in the back of the classroom in a well-run online course.

Mixing the Technologies

Many courses use a combination of technologies as well as print materials. For example, at Southwest Texas State University, a course in geography for elementary and high school teachers begins with a videoconference, with the instructor introducing himself or herself and outlining the course requirements. A printed study guide with all assigned readings and activities is distributed to all participants at the first session. Teachers who cannot get to a videoconferencing site are sent a videocassette of the first session along with the study guide. After the first session, the course moves on line. Using chat rooms, threaded discussions, and e-mail, participants do their assignments and group

The time and place dimensions of various distance learning instructional technologies.

	Specific place	Any place
Any time (asynchronous)		◆ Online courses (newsgroups, bulletin boards, websites, e-mail) ◆ CD ROMs, DVDs ◆ Videotapes ◆ Audiotapes ◆ Correspondence courses
Specific time (synchronous)	◆ Two-way interactive videoconferencing ◆ Two-way interactive audioconferencing ◆ Traditional on-campus classes	◆ Online course (interactive computer conferencing, chat rooms, MUDs, MOOs) ◆ Radio broadcasts ◆ TV broadcasts, satellite, and cable

projects and interact on line. Assignments are snail-mailed to the faculty member. Finally, the class concludes with another synchronous videoconference or recorded videotape.

This course may be unusual in that it combines two of the major distance learning technologies, but it is not unusual to find courses that use one of the major technologies and supplement it with another. For example, e-mail is used for individual student-instructor communication in most courses, even if the course is conducted by two-way interactive videotape or prerecorded video.

Future Trends

Today, online instruction, two-way interactive video, and one-way prerecorded video are the most popular instructional technologies in distance education. According to the Department of Education's National Center for Education Statistics, colleges and universities are planning to increase their use of Internet-based instruction and two-way interactive video. Prerecorded video is likely to decrease in popularity. The explosive growth in distance learning in the last five years has come primarily from online courses, and that is likely to continue. With better databases and other sources of information continuing to appear on the Internet, ease of access to reliable data will increase. As high bandwidth connections to the Internet start to replace phone connections, the capacity to quickly transmit large amounts of data will increase dramatically. For example, with a high-speed modem and phone connection, it can take several minutes to download a video snippet. Thus, most online courses today use text, images, and perhaps some animation, but they are limited in their video capabilities. Eventually, high bandwidth technologies will make individualized, customized, and live video interactions possible, with lengthy video programming available. Online distance learning is also causing a shift to a more collaborative learning model. "Because of the nature of online resources and communication, the faculty is no longer the one authoritative voice," explains Claudine SchWeber of the University of Maryland University College. An undergraduate there agrees. "Students learn from each other as well as from the instructor and course materials," she commented. "Instructors who are comfortable with online technology . . . create a classroom environment that is interactive, inviting, stimulating, motivating, and lively." Another interesting trend to note is the incorporation of the new instructional technologies in conventional, classroom-based courses. "What we are finding is that our distance technology is having an impact on the way we teach on-campus courses to undergraduate and graduate students," comments McRae C. Banks, head of the department of management and professor of entrepreneurship at Worcester Polytechnic Institute in Massachusetts. "As one example, some faculty members have students take online quizzes before each class period . . . . Before the professor goes into class, he or she knows what areas the students understand and what areas are troubling them. Now more time can be spent where the students are having difficulty." Other professors hold office hours or help sessions in chat rooms when they are at home or out of town at

"What we are finding is that our distance technology is having an impact on the way we teach on-campus courses to undergraduate and graduate students," comments McRae C. Banks of Worcester Polytechnic Institute.

conferences. Still others require students to respond to each class lecture by posting a comment to a discussion group. "For us, the bottom line is finding ways to enhance the educational experience for students," says Banks.

WHAT CAN YOU LEARN VIA DISTANCE EDUCATION?

The short answer is almost anything. You can take a single course in almost any field, or earn a certificate or degree in many fields, by distance education. Next, we'll give you an overview of what's available, and in Chapter 3 we'll discuss these programs in more detail.

Course Offerings

According to the National Center for Education Statistics, an estimated 54,470 different distance education courses were offered in academic year 1997–1998, the last year for which reliable figures are available. That number has undoubtedly increased considerably since then. As you can see in Figure 1-1, most of these courses were college-level, credit-granting courses at the undergraduate level, and about one quarter were at the graduate/first professional level. Fewer than one tenth were noncredit-granting courses.

According to Figure 1-2, of the courses offered, the greatest number can be found in fields that are part of a general undergraduate education, such as English, humanities, and the social and behavioral sciences; physical and life sciences; and mathematics. However, in the fields of education, engineering, and library and information sciences, more courses are offered at the graduate/first-professional level than at the undergraduate level. According to the Department of Education, there are three likely reasons for this: the emphasis on graduate education in these fields, the suitability of course content for distance education, and the likelihood that groups of students would be located in particular places, such as a school district or engineering firm, to receive broadcast or interactive video courses.

Figure 1–1: Distance Education Course Offerings in 1997–1998 (by level)

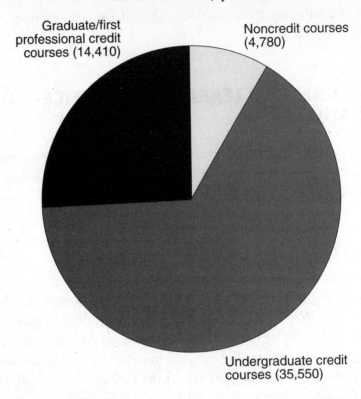

Graduate/first professional credit courses (14,410)

Noncredit courses (4,780)

Undergraduate credit courses (35,550)

Source: Data from U.S. Department of Education, National Center for Education Statistics, Postsecondary Education Quick Information System, *Survey on Distance Education at Postsecondary Education Institutions*, 1998-1999, p. 19.

Degree and Certificate Programs

Many institutions of higher learning simply offer a smorgasbord of distance education courses that can be taken for credit. An increasing number of institutions, however, have taken distance education to the next step; they have begun to offer undergraduate and graduate certificate and degree programs that can be completed entirely by distance education. For example, a student with an associate's degree from a local community college can go on to earn a baccalaureate degree from a four-year institution by distance learning, without relocating. Or a

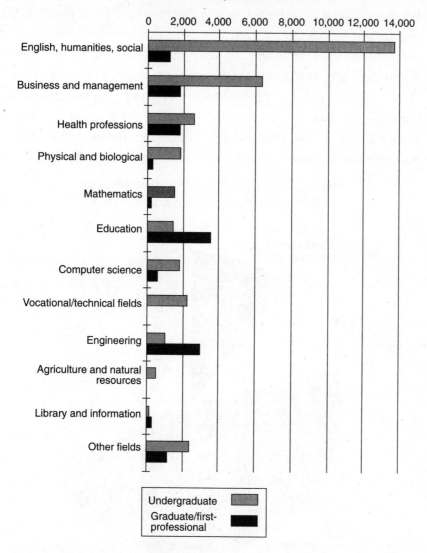

Figure 1–2: Distance Education Course Offerings by Field of Study, 1997–1998

Source: Data from U.S. Department of Education, National Center for Education Statistics, Postsecondary Education Quick Information System, *Survey on Distance Education at Postsecondary Education Institutions*, 1998-1999, p. 25.

Forecasters at International Data Corporation predict that there will be 2.23 million students taking higher-education distance learning courses by the year 2002 (out of 15.1 million students overall), up from 710,000 distance learners in 1998 (out of 14.6 million students overall).

Peterson's *Guide to Distance Learning Programs: 2001* lists almost 3,000 degree and certificate programs, representing a phenomenal increase in the last few years.

working professional can earn a master's degree or professional certificate on a part-time basis through distance learning. According to the

National Center on Education Statistics, in 1997–1998, there were an estimated 1,230 degree programs available through distance learning. Peterson's *Guide to Distance Learning Programs: 2001* lists about 3,000 degree and certificate programs, so you can see there has been a phenomenal increase in the last few years. Unlike individual course offerings, degree and certificate programs are more likely to be offered at the graduate and first-professional level than at the undergraduate level, as you can see in Figure 1-3. Most degree and certificate programs are in the fields of liberal/general studies, business and management, health professions, education, and engineering.

Figure 1–3: Distance Education Degree and Certificate Programs, 1997–1998

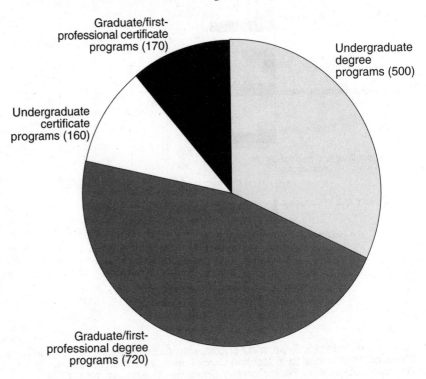

Source: Data from U.S. Department of Education, National Center for Education Statistics, Postsecondary Education Quick Information System, *Survey on Distance Education at Postsecondary Education Institutions*, 1998-1999, p. 34.

WHO OFFERS DISTANCE LEARNING?

The better question might be, "Who doesn't?" With lifelong learning becoming commonplace and communications technologies improving rapidly, the demand for distance education has grown dramatically, and with it the number and variety of providers. The first group of providers consists of the traditional colleges, universities, graduate schools, community colleges, technical schools, and vocational schools. These providers range from schools only their neighbors have heard of to household names like Stanford, Virginia Tech, and the University of California, to name just a few. The challenges posed by distance education have forced colleges and universities to be creative in their approaches. Some schools have formed partnerships with cable companies, public broadcasting services, satellite broadcasters, and online education companies to deliver high-quality distance education. Colleges and universities also partner with corporations to deliver courses and degree programs to employees. For example, the University of Cincinnati's College of Pharmacy offers courses and a master's degree program via distance learning to employees of Procter & Gamble Pharmaceuticals Norwich, New York, location as well as other P&G sites.

Many schools have formed consortia, or collaborative groups, within a state or region or even internationally, which enables students to take courses as needed from all the participating institutions. An example of a consortium is the University of Texas (UT) TeleCampus, which does not confer degrees but supports the participating University of Texas campuses, which do award degrees.

A few colleges and universities are virtual, meaning they don't have a campus. These schools offer most or all of their instruction by means of distance education, providing complete degree programs. The University of Phoenix Online and Walden University are two well-known examples.

> **The three most common subjects taught by distance education are social sciences, business, and education; followed closely by computer science and health.**

Finally, there are many online purveyors of noncredit distance education courses on subjects that range from candlemaking and beauty secrets to C++ programming and Spanish. These courses may be fun and even instructive, but they won't contribute to your formal educational credentials.

We'll discuss the providers of distance education more fully in Chapter 4.

HOW EFFECTIVE IS DISTANCE LEARNING?

There is a great deal of interest in the effectiveness of distance learning. Research into this subject is largely anecdotal and much of it is out-of-date, given the rapid development of instructional technology in the last few years. However, Thomas L. Russell, in a widely quoted report entitled *The No Significant Difference Phenomenon*, concluded from a review of 355 research studies and summaries published between 1928 and 1999 that the learning outcomes (test scores and course grades) of distance learning and traditional students are similar. In addition, Russell found that distance learners themselves have positive attitudes toward distance education and are generally satisfied with it. There are a number of questions regarding the effectiveness of distance education that have not yet been answered by the research. For example, how do the different learning styles of students relate to the use of particular technologies? How do individual differences among students affect their ability to learn by distance education? Why do more students drop out of distance education courses than drop out of traditional courses? What types of content are most suitable for distance learning? Common sense suggests that distance education is more effective for some people than for others, the different instructional technologies are more effective with different types of learners, and some subjects are more suitable for distance education than other subjects.

Some educators are not fans of distance education, believing that technology, no matter how sophisticated, cannot substitute the face-to-face interactions of a community of teachers and learners. Even

According to a report entitled *The No Significant Difference Phenomenon*, the learning outcomes (test scores and course grades) of distance learning and traditional students are similar.

proponents of distance learning concede that students who have the time and money for a traditional on-campus education should go for it. "Technology can't provide the intangible experiences of campus life, especially on the undergraduate level," comments Robert V. Steiner, who directs the distance learning project at Columbia University's Teachers College. "However, distance education is extremely helpful for adult learners who need to get their education in a flexible manner."

Barbara Lockee, Virginia Tech's distance learning program developer and an assistant professor of instructional technology, agrees. "Distance education has the increased potential to reach new audiences that haven't had access to higher education," says Lockee. "Because of the changing needs of our work force, people who are employed need on-going, lifelong education. So new higher-ed participants are in their 30s and beyond, and many probably have their undergraduate degree but need skills to be successful in the information age."

Distance education may have benefits beyond accessibility, flexibility, and convenience. For example, when asked to compare the experiences of teaching a course to a single classroom of students and by two-way interactive video, Larry Anthony indicated that the students in the distance learning course had the richer experience. "We were hearing from people in different parts of the country," he explained. "In addiction studies, there are different cultural issues and problems in different places. In terms of diversity, the distance learning class was great." Kevin Ruthen, who earned a Master of Science degree in information resource management from Syracuse University, also thought that distance education had added to the value of his degree: "The students and professors . . . were all different ages, from many professional fields, and from many regions of the world," he recalls. "I learned a tremendous amount and gained many different perspectives due to this diversity as opposed to what would be, in my opinion, a less diverse class environment in an on-campus class."

"I learned a tremendous amount and gained many different perspectives due to this diversity as opposed to what would be, in my opinion, a less diverse class environment in an on-campus class," reports distance learner Kevin Ruthen.

PURSUING YOUR EDUCATION BY DISTANCE LEARNING

Still interested in distance learning? Then the next question is: What's involved in finding a reputable distance education program and getting in? A lot. The first, and perhaps the most important part of this process, is a combination of introspection and research. You are going to have to assess yourself and what's out there to find a good match. You'll have to answer questions like: What are my professional goals? What are my interests and abilities? Which courses or certificate or degree programs will help me achieve my goals? Am I prepared for higher education in this field? What must I do to improve my qualifications? Do I have the motivation, personal characteristics, and skills that will enable me to learn at a distance? In Chapter 2, we will help you assess the advantages and disadvantages of distance learning as well as your strengths and weaknesses; this will enable you to decide whether or not distance education is for you. Then in Chapter 3, we'll describe the different degree and certificate programs that are available, what's involved in transferring credits, and how you may be able to earn credits for prior learning and life experience. In Chapter 4 we'll describe the various types of distance learning providers. We'll give you suggestions on how to find out more about programs and institutions.

Once you've done your research on distance education programs, on what basis should you evaluate them? In addition to finding out the all-important accreditation status of the programs in which you are interested, you'll have to find out what each program is really like and whether it's a good match for you. Will the program help you achieve your educational and professional goals? Is the instructional technology a comfortable match for you? Chapter 5 discusses these issues and provides a checklist of factors you should consider when you evaluate distance education programs.

Once you've identified the programs to which you will apply, what standardized qualifying exams, if any, will you need to take? What should you do to prepare for the Scholastic Aptitude Test (SAT), Graduate Record Examinations (GRE), or one of the graduate admissions examinations used by many of the professional schools? You will have to find out what each program requires as part of its application and what the deadlines are. You may have to write a personal statement so that the admissions committee can evaluate your background. You will have to ask instructors or colleagues to write letters of recommendation. In Chapters 6 and 7 we'll describe the process in more detail and give you suggestions on how to prepare applications that will gain you admission.

How are you going to pay for your education? If you are planning to attend part-time while working, that may not be a problem. But for full-time students, financing a distance degree program can be complicated. You will have to figure out how much money you will need, find possible sources of aid, and apply for them. Chapter 8 covers financing your distance education.

Finally, in Chapter 9, some of the students we interviewed and surveyed will share more of their experiences and offer additional advice on succeeding in a distance education program.

In the pages that follow, there are many suggestions for accomplishing all of the tasks involved in selecting and applying to distance learning programs. Not all the advice will be applicable to everyone. Still, this book will provide you with an overview of what you will need to know. And it will indicate what you will need to find out on your own to ensure that your distance education does all that you hope it will do.

Is Distance Learning Right for You?

Chapter 2

Distance learning can satisfy a wide range of needs for many people in diverse circumstances, but it's not for everyone. Some students don't have the study skills or self-discipline to succeed as a distance learner. Others are interested in a field of study or a degree that is not offered via distance learning. Still, for most people distance learning has the potential to open up new possibilities in higher education. For many adult students, the advantages of distance learning far outweigh the disadvantages. In this chapter, we'll discuss the pros and cons of distance learning and help you assess whether or not distance learning is right for you.

THE ADVANTAGES OF DISTANCE LEARNING

Distance learning has many benefits. That's why distance-learning programs meet the needs of so many different people of all ages, genders, professions, and educational backgrounds.

As you read the following list of distance learning benefits, ask yourself if any of them provide a way to overcome an obstacle that is standing in your way when you think about going back to school. Do any of these advantages make continuing your education a real possibility right now, rather than a vague goal for sometime in the future?

Here are the benefits of distance learning in general:

- **Distance learning breaks down time barriers.** In most distance learning programs, you don't have to be at a certain place at a certain time. You can learn when it's convenient for you, so you can fit your education into a busy work and home life. You only take as many courses as you can handle at a time, and sometimes you can start whenever you like instead of at the beginning of a semester.

Game Plan for Distance Learning

- **Distance learning breaks down geographical barriers.** Whether you are logging on to a course from your own computer at home or traveling a short distance to a satellite classroom, distance education makes your geographical distance from a college or university irrelevant. Students who live in remote areas, who don't have time to commute to a campus, and who travel a lot on business benefit from this aspect of distance education.

- **Distance learning goes at your own pace.** Distance learning is ideal for students who like to set their own pace and who learn best on their own. As you work through course material, you can spend more time on difficult concepts and less time on easier ones. Although you are likely to have weekly or other periodic deadlines, as long as you make them, you can approach the work at a pace that suits your schedule.

- **Distance learning can save money.** Although the tuition and fees for distance learning courses are usually comparable to those charged for on-campus courses, you can save money on child care, gas, parking, and other commuting costs. In addition, you generally don't have to take time off from work to attend class.

- **Distance learning fits individual needs.** You can often tailor a program to fit your particular educational and professional goals and take courses from various institutions if necessary.

- **Distance learning provides freedom of choice.** Since you are not confined to schools within easy commuting distance, you are able to consider distance learning programs at reputable colleges and universities around the country and the world.

- **Distance learning teaches more than just the course material.** Depending on the type of program you take, distance learning can improve your computer, Internet, reading, writing, and oral communication skills, which benefits you no matter what kind of career you pursue.

- **Distance learning broadens your perspective.** Often, your classmates will be from diverse backgrounds and places. You will interact with a more diverse group of people than you would normally find on most campuses.

Refer to Figure 2-1 for the specific advantages of each of the major distance learning instructional technologies.

Specific Advantages and Disadvantages of the Major Distance Learning Technologies

Distance Learning Technology	Advantages	Disadvantages
Online	▲Course work can be done at any time of day or night. ▲Any computer with Internet access can be used. ▲Courses can easily be taken from more than one school. ▲Computer skills are developed. ▲There are no commuting costs.	▼Lots of self-discipline and motivation are needed. ▼A computer with Internet access is needed—a significant cost. ▼Social interaction is on line only.
Two-way interactive videoconferencing	▲There is access to courses at distant campuses. ▲Social interaction is most similar to that of a traditional classroom. ▲There is no cost to the student for technology.	▼Classes are held at particular times and places.
Videotapes of class sessions	▲Course work can be done at any time of day or night. ▲Any TV and VCR can be used. ▲There are no commuting costs.	▼Lots of self-discipline and motivation are needed. ▼Social interaction is minimal. ▼Distance learners are several days behind on-campus class.

THE DISADVANTAGES OF DISTANCE LEARNING

Lest you think that distance learning is the solution to all problems of access to education, it does have its drawbacks. Consider whether or not any of the following general disadvantages would cause you to eliminate distance learning from your education plans. For disadvantages specific to a particular instructional technology, refer to Figure 2-1.

- **Distance learning requires a high degree of discipline and self-motivation.** Dropout rates are higher for distance learning programs than for campus-based programs. No doubt, some dropouts are students who did not realize that distance learning requires as much, if not more, time than a traditional on-campus class. For older distance education students, it's easy for work or family needs to take priority over education. Many distance learners drop out because the distance course is the easiest thing to let go of when things get too hectic.

- **Distance learning can be lonely.** Some people need the face-to-face interaction that a traditional classroom provides. Even though instructors may try to overcome social isolation in distance learning courses, for some students there is simply not enough social contact to keep them enthusiastic and motivated.

- **Distance learning can take longer.** Because distance learning is self-motivated, it's easier to give in to other demands on your time and postpone taking courses, increasing the time it takes to complete a degree program.

- **Distance learning students may get poor student services.** On-campus students have convenient access to the library, academic advisers, job placement services, tutoring, and student centers. Many distance learning programs offer student services such as online library access and registration, but in most schools the services still can't compare to those available to on-campus students.

- **Distance learning students miss the college experience.** College campuses offer a lot more than classes, with cultural and sports activities, dorm life, faculty-student interaction, and the opportunity to form lifelong friendships. Although this is not an important consideration for most older distance learners, younger students that pursue an undergraduate education may find the on-campus experience too valuable to pass up.

- **A traditional college degree is a better choice to meet some future goals.** Although distance learning is becoming more mainstream and is usually accepted by employers, as long as it is from a reputable institution, it is still regarded by some in the traditional academic community as inferior. Thus, a traditional degree may be more valuable if you are considering applying in the future to the more prestigious graduate and professional programs, including law school and medical school.

ASSESSING YOURSELF

With the advantages and disadvantages of distance learning in mind, you should take some time to honestly answer the following questions. Consider your own goals, circumstances, personality, skills, social support, and comfort with technology to determine whether or not you are a good candidate for distance learning.

Goals

What are your educational and professional goals?

First you must determine your educational and professional goals. Ask yourself what you would like to be doing in five or ten years, and then determine what courses or degree programs will help you achieve your goals. Do you need a course to update your skills, a certificate to provide professional credentials, or a degree to solidify or advance your professional standing?

For example, when Head Start announced that an associate's degree in early childhood education would soon be a requirement for its teachers, Angela Butcher had a problem. Butcher, who teaches at Jackson-Vinton Community Action Head Start in Ohio, just had a high school diploma. "I was so scared of losing my job. Going to a college campus (the closest is 45 minutes away) after working 8 hours a day and finding a sitter for my two children because my husband works second shift—it was just impossible to even think about doing it. Then my director received a brochure about the distance learning program at the University of Cincinnati and asked if I would like to give college a shot that way." Butcher continues, "I felt this was a true gift to help me to [keep] the profession that is dear to me."

For Butcher, the goal was crystal clear and the means of achieving that goal fell into place quite nicely. However, for any student, it's important to know what you hope to accomplish by undertaking any

"Make sure you have your goals defined," says Scott Garrod. "Then the decision between a distance or traditional [program] will be easy."

"The online program . . . offers me maximum flexibility in which to pursue my educational goals without interfering with the rest of my crazy schedule."

degree program. "Make sure you have your goals defined," advises Scott Garrod, a Master of Business candidate at Syracuse University. "Then the decision between a distance or traditional [program] will be easy." Keep in mind that in some fields a distance education degree is not as acceptable as it is in others. Although most business employers don't make any distinctions between distance and on-campus degrees, as long as they are from reputable institutions, in academia and some professions employers may not be so accommodating. Be sure you understand what academic credentials will carry weight in the field in which you are interested.

Why are you considering distance education?

Do you have a busy schedule full of commitments to work, family, and community? If so, your top reason for enrolling in a distance education course or program may be the flexibility it offers. The ability to do course work at your own convenience is the key consideration for most distance learners.

"My schedule does not permit consistent attendance in a traditional classroom," comments one 46-year-old undergraduate. "As a consultant, I may be required to spend up to 60 hours at a client site . . . . As a parent, I have many commitments that would take priority over my attending class." She continues, "The online program at the University of Maryland University College offers me maximum flexibility in which to pursue my educational goals without interfering with the rest of my crazy schedule." Another student, Kimberly Foreman, who is studying for a Master of Healthcare Administration from Seton Hall University's online program in New Jersey, investigated several programs. "Traditional on-campus evening classes interfered with work and family obligations. The weekend programs still required that I be at a certain place at a certain time, and this was also inconvenient," she explains. "I wanted flexibility and a program that allowed me to be self-directed but still have interaction with faculty members and classmates." The online program she found at Seton Hall met her needs.

Some students need the flexibility of distance education because their work involves a great deal of travel. "With my job, travel is a requirement . . . sometimes unpredictable travel," says Scott Garrod of Syracuse University. "So a distance learning program that was not classroom-dependent was a great alternative." Another student, Paul Nashawaty, explains, "My profession has me traveling around and moving from place to place." Nashawaty, who is earning a Master of Business Administration from Worcester Polytechnic Institute in Massachusetts, concluded, "It would be very difficult for me to transfer from school to school."

Other students enroll in distance education courses and programs because they live too far from the institutions of higher learning that offer the education they need. These are students for whom the word "distance" in distance learning has a literal meaning. "My husband is a farmer, so my family is not mobile," explains Patti Iversen, a nurse who lives in Montana and is working on a Master of Science in Nursing degree (family nurse practitioner) from Gonzaga University in Spokane, Washington. "I live in a rural community and the closest colleges and universities are 250 to 300 miles from my home. I did not want to leave my family for extended periods of time in order to meet my educational and career objectives." For Iversen, distance learning was the only way to achieve her goals.

"I wanted a degree from a respected and vigorous program but didn't want to move my family or quit my job," says Lara Hollenczer, a marketing manager who lives in Maryland and is pursuing a master's degree in communications management from Syracuse University in New York. Distance learning provided Hollenczer the means to earn the degree she wanted without disrupting her work and family life. So, when you consider taking a course or enrolling in a degree program, ask yourself whether flexibility of time and place is critical for you. If flexibility is one of your top needs, distance learning may be the right choice for you.

"I wanted a degree from a respected and vigorous program but didn't want to move my family or quit my job," says Lara Hollenczer.

Personal Attitudes and Skills

Are you prepared to do as much work as you would have to do in a traditional course, and perhaps more?
Many people believe that distance learning is an easier or faster way to earn a degree. This is because in recent years many fraudulent distance-learning schools have sprung up, promising degrees in little or no time for little or no work. These diploma mills have given rise to the false

perception that distance learning degrees are somehow easier to earn than degrees earned the traditional way. However, distance learning courses and degree programs offered by reputable schools require just as much time and effort as their on-campus counterparts.

"Some students think that an online course is cybersurfing for credit," says Michael S. Ameigh, Assistant Provost for Distance Learning and Information Resources and Associate Professor of Communication Studies at the State University of New York at Oswego. "But an online course is actually more work than if students took the course in the classroom." That's because online instructors often require a certain amount of participation from students in order to pass the course, whereas most classroom instructors do not demand participation from students beyond completing the assignments and exams. So, at the beginning of each course, Ameigh tries to weed out students who think that online learning is easier than conventional courses. He provides a six-minute "welcome document," a streaming media PowerPoint presentation with narration that gives an overview of what the course covers and what he expects of students. In courses taken by distance learners and on-campus students, instructors make no distinctions between distance learners and traditional students when it comes to the course work that they must do. For example, in Gonzaga University's undergraduate and graduate nursing programs, "Course requirements for students at a distance are identical to those for their on-campus colleagues," according to Dale Ann Abendroth, Assistant Professor of Nursing.

From the student's perspective, a high-quality distance education course is as rigorous as a traditional course. "Certainly the expectations of the instructor and the volume of readings and assignments were as stringent, or even more so, than on-site courses I have taken," comments a high school librarian of her Rutgers University postgraduate course in critical issues for the wired classroom. "Be prepared for a great deal of work. It seems to me that more work is assigned than in a 'regular' class, so students shouldn't perceive distance learning as an easy way out. It isn't!"

> **"Some students think that an online course is cybersurfing for credit," says Professor Michael S. Ameigh.**

> **"It seems to me that more work is assigned than in a 'regular' class, so students shouldn't perceive distance learning as an easy way out. It isn't!"**

Do you have the time-management skills necessary to juggle work, home, and school responsibilities?

As we have seen, a distance learning course or program takes as much time as a traditional one, and sometimes more. So ask yourself, do you have enough time to take a distance learning course or courses? Will you be able to juggle your course work, professional work, family obligations, and community activities to make time for all your responsibilities? "I've seen students register for four or five classes in a semester and try to work full-time," says Patti Wolf, Assistant Academic Director and Assistant Professor of Computer Science at the University of Maryland University College. "Many of these students have underestimated the time required for their online courses and ended up doing poorly." Wolf adds, "You should expect to spend as much time on line (or otherwise preparing for class) as you would in a traditional classroom." Distance learner Patti Iversen advises students to "be realistic about the amount of time that will be needed for study and travel, if required [for programs with residency periods]."

In addition to having enough time to do the course work, students have to be able to plan their time, make a schedule, and stick to it. "The biggest problem I see among my students is an inability to budget their time," says Wolf. "They get to the third week of class and realize that it's Saturday night and they haven't done their homework."

Iversen agrees. "Failure to adequately anticipate and plan for the rigors of independent learning leads to frustration and poor outcomes," she warns. Even though many courses, like Wolf's, are set up in weekly blocks to help students pace themselves, it's still up to the student to make time to log on or watch the videotape and do the assignments.

Do you have the discipline and self-motivation to work regularly if you don't have to show up for class at a given time and place?

When we asked students and faculty members what personal qualities a distance learner needs, most people mentioned discipline and self-motivation as the keys to success. "Success as a distance learner requires more self-discipline and greater ability to learn autonomously than site-based learning," claims distance learner Patti Iversen. M.B.A. candidate Paul Nashawaty echoes her remarks, "You must keep on top of the workload and try not to slack off," he says. "Discipline is my number-one factor for success in this program." A University of Maryland University College undergraduate agrees, "Students [must] have the discipline to complete course work studies and assignments on time and independently without the in-person reminders that come with regularly scheduled class meetings." When you are considering distance education, ask yourself whether or not you have the qualities needed to see it through. According to Denise Petrosino, a certified public accountant working on a master's in organizational management from the University of Phoenix Online, "As long as you are goal-oriented and self-motivated, you can do it."

Do you have the initiative and assertiveness needed to succeed in a distance learning environment?

Initiative and assertiveness are qualities needed for success in distance learning. Students need to take the initiative to ask questions and resolve problems that the instructor may not be able to perceive.

In addition, students in distance learning courses need to be assertive in order to make themselves known to the instructor and to other students. For example, in an online course, a student who never participates in threaded discussions tends to "disappear." "In the online environment, students have to be assertive," says Michael S. Ameigh of the State University of New York at Oswego. "Otherwise we don't know who they are." Similarly, in a prerecorded video course, a student who never contacts the instructor has little presence in the instructor's mind. Of course, initiative and assertiveness are pluses for traditional on-campus students, too. The student who speaks up in class is more likely to have a good learning experience and succeed in a course than the student who sits silently in the back of the room. For many adults, maturity brings assertiveness. "My students are a professional group," says Dale Ann Abendroth, Assistant Professor of Nursing at Gonzaga University. "It's rare that I have a wallflower in a course."

Your Academic and Professional Skills

Do you have sound study skills, including reading, researching, writing papers, and taking exams?

Good study skills are a necessary prerequisite for distance learning. In fact, many institutions that offer distance learning courses and degree programs require that students have taken at least some college-level courses before they enroll in a distance education degree program. For example, some distance education bachelor's programs prefer students with an associate's degree from a community college or a certain minimum number of undergraduate credit hours. In this way, they ensure that students are ready to tackle course work via distance learning without needing much help with basic study skills.

For graduate programs, it is simply assumed that students have the necessary study skills and are ready to undertake graduate-level work. Laurie Noe, a doctoral candidate in management of children and youth programs at Nova Southeastern University, explains, "You are required to produce papers, take tests, conduct research, and formulate and state your opinions just as if you were in a traditional setting."

Do you have good communication skills? Can you present yourself well in writing? Can you speak up on camera?

Good communication skills—reading, writing, listening, and speaking—are necessary to succeed in all types of distance learning courses and programs. However, different distance learning technologies emphasize different communication skills.

"Online students have to be reasonably articulate in the written mode of communication," explains Claudine SchWeber, Assistant Vice President for Distance Education and Lifelong Learning at the University of Maryland University College. That's because virtually all communication in an online course takes place through the written word, therefore you must be comfortable with reading messages and responding in writing.

For some people, this is ideal. "Students who are petrified to talk in class often find it easy to communicate in writing on line. They can make well-reasoned, thought-out responses to the discussion," explains Patti Wolf of the University of Maryland University College. "One of the things that happens on line is that people who talk little in the classroom feel more comfortable and tend to communicate well on line," says Karen Novick, Director of Professional Development Studies at Rutgers University in New Jersey. Robert V. Steiner, who directs the distance learning project at Teachers College, Columbia University, also agrees. "For some students, online learning may provide a

"People who talk little in the classroom feel more comfortable and tend to communicate well on line," says Karen Novick of Rutgers University.

more comfortable environment in which to express themselves. Students can reflect on what they want to say before they post a message." On the other hand, some students are simply more visual and more oriented to getting information via television rather than the written word. For them, two-way interactive video is a more comfortable way to communicate. It's easier for these students to speak up and communicate with people they can see and hear rather than to write messages to unseen students and instructors. "Once students get used to being on camera, they react fairly normally," says Larry Anthony, Director of the Addiction Studies Program at the University of Cincinnati. Of course, students who take courses via video still need written communication skills because most of their assignments and exams are in writing.

If you are pursuing a degree or certificate to improve your professional standing, do you have the background that may be required?

Many graduate-level professional programs require that students have worked in the field for several years before they apply. For example, many programs that offer a Master in Business Administration prefer students who have demonstrated their professional capabilities through several years of work. Graduate-level work in other fields, such as nursing, social work, and education, often requires related work experience. Be sure you have the necessary professional background for the programs you are considering.

Social Factors

Do you have the support of your family and employers?

As you have realized by now, a distance learning course or program can be challenging. Taking such a course or program means that you will be working harder than ever, so having the backing of your family and employer can be very helpful. "It's important to have a good support group behind you," says Barbara Rosenbaum, who is working on a master's degree in communications management from Syracuse University. "My husband, friends, family, and colleagues helped me keep my energy and focus up." Distance learner Patti Iversen agrees. "A local support network is a valuable asset in helping to overcome the occasional slump in motivation that occurs over time."

**Are you comfortable with the social interaction that is
characteristic of distance learning? Can you overcome or
accept the social isolation that often occurs?**

The issue of social interaction and isolation is complex because different factors, including instructional technology, personality, and life
circumstances, influence how each person reacts to the social element
of distance learning.

Instructional technology. As we saw when we discussed communication skills, each distance learning technology draws on particular skills.
Similarly, each distance learning technology offers a different type of
social interaction. Let's look at each major distance learning technology to get a better idea of how it affects the social elements of
distance education.

The technology that offers a social experience most similar to that
of the conventional classroom is two-way interactive video. Even
though the students may be geographically distant from one another,
communication is in real time, people can see one another, and the
feeling of social isolation is minimized. Kenneth Wachter, Professor of
Demography at the University of California at Berkeley, offered an
advanced postgraduate course in mathematical demography via two-
way interactive video to students at Berkeley and the University of
California at Los Angeles. He was delighted by how the two groups of
students were brought together. "The thing that works best is the
human back and forth," says Wachter.

Online courses can also offer social interaction, but in a new and,
to some, unfamiliar form. "At first it is strange e-mailing someone you
don't know. However, you get to know the person via e-mail just as you
would talking or writing a letter," explains an undergraduate at the
University of Maryland University College. "In the cybercafes that are
provided for classmates, we talk about class work, movies, music, time
management, and sports. It helps bring the class together socially."
Denise Petrosino, who is enrolled in a master's program in organizational management at the University of Phoenix Online, agrees. "If you
have a fear of limited interaction with the teacher and students, you can
put that aside because I believe that we learn more about our teacher
and classmates in the online program than in the live classroom," says

"At first it is strange e-mailing someone you don't know. However, you get to know the person via e-mail just as you would talking or writing a letter."

"Eye contact, vocal inflection, body language—all these elements of communication are missing [on line]," explains Robert V. Steiner of Teachers College, Columbia University.

Petrosino. "The reason I say this is because you get to read all correspondence between students and teacher."

In courses in which class videotapes are mailed to off-site students, the sense of social isolation is the most pronounced. That's because these courses often do not provide a means for ongoing discussion between off-site students, on-site students, and instructors. "The professors do not know much about the distance students' personalities, or even what they look like," explains Nicole DeRaleau, who lives in Connecticut and is a Master of Engineering student at Worcester Polytechnic Institute in Massachusetts. "Their interaction with us is minimal, and the closest form of personal interaction may be a telephone call, which is almost always initiated by the student." Note that some courses that rely on videotapes for instructional delivery are now moving on line as well, establishing class bulletin boards on which discussions can take place, thus improving the social interaction of the off-site students.

Personality. The second factor that influences how social interaction and social isolation are perceived is an individual's personality—one person's social isolation is another person's cherished privacy. For some people, the type of interaction that characterizes distance learning is not enough to overcome a sense of social isolation. "Eye contact, vocal inflection, body language—all these elements of communication are missing [on line]," explains Robert V. Steiner, who directs the distance learning project at Teachers College, Columbia University. "For some people, the sense of isolation can be significant." Joanne Simon, a student at the University of Phoenix Online who actually prefers online classes to traditional classes, admits, "I like to talk, so for me, the social interaction is lacking." Another distance learner thinks that people who are "social butterflies" will find the social interactions of distance learning unfulfilling.

On the other hand, people who are not especially extroverted may find distance learning suits them. They can participate, especially in online courses, without risking too much personal revelation.

Personal circumstances. How important is social interaction? Clearly, there must be enough interaction to facilitate learning. But for many adult students, the lack of social interaction is simply not a problem.

"For the most part, I feel detached from the class itself, and that is okay," says Brigit Dolan, a nurse who lives in Boise, Idaho, and is enrolled in Gonzaga University's Master of Science in Nursing program in Spokane, Washington. In this program, students are required to attend classes three times per semester. The remaining classes are mailed to them on videotape. "I feel okay to share my ideas and experiences when I'm there, but I'm fulfilled enough in other areas of my life that I don't yearn for that much interaction from my school life .... I just do my work, communicate with my professors and classmates occasionally, and that's about it." Like Brigit Dolan, most adult students are not looking for the social life and collegiality that are characteristics of the on-campus undergraduate experience. A librarian taking a postgraduate course at Rutgers University explains, "I don't think social interaction is a high priority in the kind of postgrad courses I take; we all have jobs and personal lives, and time is precious." Carla Gentry, a nurse enrolled in a distance learning master's program, agrees. "At my stage in life, I am not going to school for the social benefits."

"I don't think social interaction is a high priority in the kind of postgrad courses I take: we all have jobs and personal lives, and time is precious."

How well do you work with others?

After the discussion of social interaction and social isolation, you may wonder why working well with others is important in the distance learning environment. The reason is that many instructors try to overcome the potential social isolation of the distance education course by assigning group work, thus forcing people to interact with each other.

Doing a group project in a distance learning class is challenging. The first challenge is to coordinate the activities of a group of people who are extremely busy, geographically distant from one another, and doing their work at different hours of the day and night. The second challenge is to get a group of distance learners to work together. "Since distance learners are so independent and self-motivated, they also like to do things their own way," says Brigit Dolan, who finds group projects the most challenging aspect of distance education. Trust, cooperation, and flexibility are key.

Technology Issues

Do you have the technical skills, or the willingness to acquire these skills, that may be required of a distance learning program?

Those of you who see yourselves as technologically challenged may have been dismayed by the discussion in Chapter 1 of the technology involved in many distance learning courses. Don't be. Remember that the technology is just a tool, a means to an end, and it can be learned.

In fact, some distance learning technology is not particularly advanced from the user's point of view. For example, in two-way interactive video courses, all you have to do is learn to activate the microphone (some even activate automatically when you speak) and watch the video monitors. For prerecorded video, you just pop the videocassette into the VCR and turn on the TV. Online courses do involve a little more technological savvy. However, consider the experience of one librarian who was taking a traditional on-campus postgraduate course at Rutgers University. "My first online course was thrust upon me," she recalls. The instructor, who developed a serious health problem that prevented her from coming in to class, gave students the option of continuing online. "I, on my own, would never have chosen this mode; I was too computer-illiterate at that time. However, I quickly found that the technical skills required were really not onerous at all and that I could master them easily . . . . If I can succeed—no spring chicken with little technology experience—anyone can." Denise Petrosino agrees. "You do not have to be a technical genius to go to school on line. If you have a computer, can log onto the Web, and know how to use e-mail, you are set."

"You do not have to be a technical genius to go to school on line," claims Denise Petrosino.

Do you have or are you willing to gain access to the necessary equipment, which may include a computer, VCR, television, or fax machine?

Most people own a television and VCR, so these are not usually items that a new distance learner needs to purchase. However, investing in the proper computer hardware and software for a distance education program can be costly. Even if you already own a computer with Internet access, you may have to upgrade your hardware or Internet browser or purchase additional software in order to meet the minimum technical requirements of a course.

Can you tolerate dealing with technology problems?
Technology sometimes fails, and distance learners have to learn how to cope when it does. Many schools offer technical support for distance learners, and sometimes problems can be solved quickly. But if your computer system crashes for a week, you'll have to find other alternatives until you can fix the problem. "Students should be comfortable with the technology triad—fax, phone, and computer," says Claudine SchWeber of the University of Maryland University College. "Then if one goes down, they have other channels of communication."

A MINI SELF-ASSESSMENT

If you do an Internet search using the phrase "distance learning self-assessment," you will find dozens of brief quizzes designed to evaluate whether or not distance learning suits your personality, skills, and learning style. Most are posted on the Web sites of colleges and universities that offer distance education courses. For example, the University of Texas at Brownsville's distance learning self-assessment can be found at http://pubs.utb.edu/semester_courses/spring2001/distance_learnself_assessment.htm, and St. Louis Community College offers its self-assessment at http://www.stlcc.cc.mo.us/distance/assessment.

For your convenience, we've provided a brief self-assessment. Although most of the online quizzes focus on Internet-based courses, this assessment is broader. Take it and see how you do!

Distance Learning Self-Assessment

1. When I think about how I learn, I think:
   (A) I learn best independently. I am self-motivated and like to work at my own pace. I don't need a lot of handholding.
   (B) I like to work independently, but I like to get some feedback once in a while on how I'm doing. I don't need a lot of support, just a little help every once in a while.

(C) I can work independently, but I want to know where I stand. I like to be in an interactive situation where I get regular feedback on how I am doing.

(D) I need lots of interaction with my teachers and peers. I like the give and take of the classroom setting. It keeps me engaged in my classes.

2. When I think about learning through different media, such as the Internet or videoconferencing, I think:

(A) It would be exciting to be able to do my work through a different medium. The idea of sitting in a classroom does nothing for me.

(B) I am open to the idea of trying something different, like an Internet class. I would like to see how it would work for me.

(C) I'm not sure that I would be ready to work that independently. When I think of furthering my education, I see myself in a more traditional setting.

(D) I absolutely want a traditional learning experience. I want to be in a classroom setting and experience all that school has to offer.

3. When I think about interacting with my teachers, I think:

(A) I don't really care whether or not I have any face-to-face contact with my teachers. As long as I'm getting the kind of information I need to be successful in my classes, I can be satisfied as a student.

(B) I don't need a great deal of direct contact with my teachers. I'm a good, independent worker. I do want to be able to ask for help and direction when I need it.

(C) I don't need to be in a situation where I have daily conversations with my teachers, but I do like to know that they are there if I need them. I find a good teacher really helps me get excited about a topic.

(D) I really value my contacts with my teachers. I like to be able to engage in a dialogue in the classroom. A good teacher helps me connect to the subject.

4. When I think about trying to do schoolwork at home, I think:

    (A) I have a great setup at home, which is conducive to studying. I like the idea of being able to work in my own "space" and at my own pace.

    (B) I can work fairly well at home, I just have to make sure that I don't get too distracted by what is going on around me.

    (C) I could work at home, but I really don't see that as an ideal situation. There is too much going on and I would be able to concentrate better in a classroom or library setting.

    (D) There is no way I want to learn from home. I want to get out of the house and be in a classroom with other students.

5. When it comes to setting my schedule for learning and studying, I think:

    (A) I need as much flexibility as I can get. I've got a lot of other things going on in my life and I'd really like to be able to work at my own pace.

    (B) I would like to have some flexibility in scheduling my classes, but I don't want to drag it out either. I want to get through my education as quickly as possible.

    (C) I like the idea of having my time fairly structured. If I don't have someone pushing me along, it may take me longer than I want to get through school.

    (D) I need to have a structured schedule to keep me on task.

6. When I think about the traditional education experience, I think:

    (A) Campus or classroom life doesn't really appeal to me at this stage in my life. I don't need or want the experience, for example, of living in a dorm or sitting in a classroom. I want to find an alternative way of earning my degree or certificate.

    (B) I'm not sure if I want to commit to the classroom experience. It may work for me, but I'm willing to look at other ways of earning a degree.

    (C) I think I would be happier if I were on a campus somewhere. I think I'd probably regret missing out on the learning experience. I wouldn't rule out the notion of being a commuter, though.

(D) I really want a traditional learning experience where I can get away from home. I'm at a point in my life where that seems to be the logical next step for me.

To evaluate your readiness for distance education, count the number of (A)s, (B)s, (C)s, and (D)s among your responses. If most of your answers were

- (A)—you should carefully investigate distance education as an option for continuing your education.
- (B)—you should investigate whether distance learning programs are suitable for meeting at least part of your educational needs. For example, you may want to complete a significant portion of your academic work through a distance learning program but still allow yourself time for some of your work to be completed in a traditional classroom setting.
- (C)—you're probably better-suited for a traditional campus-based college experience than a distance learning environment. However, some course work through a distance learning program may be a great way to supplement your on-campus course work. You should probably look for a program that will provide you with faculty or mentor feedback on a regular basis.
- (D)—You are clearly suited for a traditional classroom setting where you can have more immediate interaction with your teachers and peers. This is not to say that you may not find distance learning programs useful at some point in the future, but it sounds like you need something more hands-on so you can get immediate feedback in the classroom while enjoying the other benefits of college life.

CONCLUSION

As you have seen in this chapter, distance learning is not for those who lack motivation or need other people to keep them on task. On the other hand, it is perfectly suited for those who have definite educational and professional goals, are committed to getting an education, are focused and organized, can persevere when things get tough, and need the flexibility that distance education offers.

Finding the time in a busy schedule to successfully complete distance learning courses is a challenge for most adults. It's easy for work and family obligations to take precedence over getting an education. Still, distance learning makes it possible for many adults who cannot regularly attend on-campus classes to get a high-quality education. As one undergraduate distance learner commented, "For working adults (and particularly working parents), distance learning may provide the best means for obtaining an undergraduate or graduate degree from a highly respected university without interfering with life's other commitments."

What Can You Study via Distance Learning?

Chapter 3

If you are interested in pursuing your education by distance learning, you are not limited to a few specialized courses or degree programs. Actually, almost every course, certificate, and degree program that you can take on campus is also available in a distance learning format. There are exceptions, of course. Degree programs in subjects that require laboratory work or performance, for example, cannot usually be done completely at a distance. Still, distance education spans a wide range of offerings, from accredited graduate-level degree programs to self-help and hobby courses. Although some programs and courses are limited to residents of certain states or regions, many are available nationwide and internationally.

In this chapter we will focus on programs and courses offered by institutions of higher education, including technical institutes, community colleges, four-year colleges, and universities. Figure 3-1 shows how higher education is structured in the United States, and how distance learning programs and courses are available at most levels of postsecondary education. The exceptions are some professional degrees, such as doctor of medicine, and postdoctoral study and research. Another partial exception is the law degree (LL.B., J.D.). Although you can acquire a law degree via distance learning, at the time this book was published, no distance learning law program has been accredited by the American Bar Association. Thus, a person with a law degree from an unaccredited distance learning program will not be able to take the bar exam in most states. The accreditation issue is important in many fields besides law, and we will examine it more closely in Chapter 5. In this chapter we'll simply give you an overview of the degrees, certificates, and courses that are available via distance learning and guidance on how to find programs and courses of interest to you.

Figure 3–1: The Structure of Higher Education in the U.S.

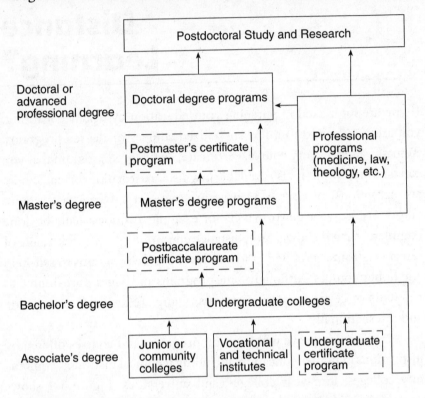

Structure of higher education in the United States. Note that the arrows indicate common pathways of students, but not the only possible pathway. *Source:* Adapted from U.S. Department of Education, National Center for Educational Statistics.

Earning credits for your past academic and other work can cut a year or more off the time it takes to earn an undergraduate degree.

UNDERGRADUATE DEGREE PROGRAMS

Today you can earn an associate's or bachelor's degree entirely by distance learning. You may also be able to shorten the time it takes to earn a degree if you transfer college credits from other institutions of higher learning, earn credits through equivalency exams, or present a portfolio of your accomplishments. For adults, earning credits for past academic and other work can cut a year or more off the time it takes to earn an undergraduate degree. So don't be shy about negotiating for credits with the school in which you plan to enroll—the time and money you save may be considerable.

Associate's Degree

The degree conferred by community colleges is the associate's degree. Students enrolled full-time can earn an associate's degree in two years, but part-time students may take much longer to earn the 60 to 64 credits required. The two most common associate's degrees are the Associate of Arts (A.A.) and the Associate of Science (A.S.), although there are many other titles that range from Associate of Business Administration (A.B.A.) to Associate of General Studies (A.G.S.). Distance learning associate's degrees are offered in a wide range of fields, including liberal arts, business, computer science, and health professions. Many students who have earned an associate's degree go on to apply those credits toward a bachelor's degree.

Bachelor's Degree

The bachelor's degree is recognized worldwide as the first university degree a student earns. In the United States, the bachelor's degree is conferred by four-year colleges, universities, and technical institutes. Although students enrolled full-time can earn the degree in four years, many actually take up to six years. Part-time students take longer, of course, to earn the 120 to 128 credits required for the bachelor's degree.

In most colleges and universities, the course of study that leads to a bachelor's degree consists of concentrated work in a "major" such as psychology or business and wide-ranging work in a variety of subjects—the liberal arts—to give students a broad foundation of knowledge. However, some bachelor's degree programs focus on intensive study in a particular field without the broad liberal arts background.

The most common bachelor's degrees are the Bachelor of Arts (B.A.) and the Bachelor of Science (B.S.), although there are scores of other titles in use as well. Distance learning bachelor's degrees are offered in many fields, including business, engineering, computer science, economics, English, history, nursing, psychology, and telecommunications. Some colleges and universities offer interdisciplinary degrees, such as environmental studies or arts management, and some permit students to design their own interdisciplinary program.

Transferring Credits

Adult students who have earned some college credits during the course of their career can decrease the time it takes to earn an undergraduate degree by transferring the credits they've earned to a degree program. Many institutions of higher learning will accept transfer credits toward a degree. *Since each school's requirements vary, it's important to check before you enroll.* The school may have rules regarding the maximum number of transfer credits and the types of courses for which credit will be granted. Consult the academic advising office before you register.

Earning Credits by Taking Exams

It's also possible to earn credit for prior learning if you take examinations to assess your knowledge and skills. For example, if you have worked in the human resources department of a large organization for years, you may know a lot about human resource management. If you take and pass a college-level exam in human resource management, you can earn 3 credits toward your degree—without taking a course or paying tuition. Although some schools have developed their own equivalency exams, most schools accept the results of examinations taken through national programs.

CLEP Exams. The most well-known of the national equivalency exam programs is the College-Level Examination Program (CLEP), which is administered by the College Entrance Examination Board and recognized by about 2,900 colleges and universities. Most of the CLEP tests are multiple-choice exams, and some are multiple-choice and essay. There are five general exams: social sciences and history, English composition, humanities, college mathematics, and natural sciences. In addition, there are about thirty specific subject area tests, including American government, Spanish, principles of management, and introductory sociology. A good score on an exam is worth between 3 and 12 credits, it depends on the exam and the credits accepted by your school. Earning credits by scoring well on equivalency exams can save you both time and tuition money. If you'd like more information about the CLEP exams, visit the College Board Web site at www.collegeboard. org/clep, e-mail them at clep@info.collegeboard.org, or call 609-771-7865.

Since each school's requirements for accepting transfer credits vary, it's very important to check how much a school will accept *before* you enroll.

Excelsior College Examinations. The Excelsior College Examination series, formerly the Regents College Examination series, is similar to the CLEP exams. The series consists of about forty subject area equivalency examinations that are 3 or 4 hours long. Subjects include anatomy and physiology, auditing, organizational behavior, and educational psychology; and the exams are recognized by almost 1,000 colleges and universities. For more information, visit the Excelsior College Web site at www.excelsior.edu, e-mail them at testadmn@ excelsior.edu, or call 888-647-2388 (toll-free).

DANTES Subject Standardized Tests. Another series of equivalency exams are the DANTES Subject Standardized Tests, or DSSTs. The DSSTs are examinations offered by The Chauncey Group International, a subsidiary of the Educational Testing Service, in trust for the United States Department of Defense as part of the military's Defense Activity for Nontraditional Education Support (DANTES). These tests were originally developed for military personnel but are now available for civilians as well. The tests are similar to the CLEP exams, but there are some subject areas not offered by CLEP, such as geography, criminal justice, marketing, technical writing, and ethics in America.

For more information about the DSSTs, you can check the Chauncey Group Web site at www.chauncey.com/dantes.html, e-mail them at dantes@chauncey.com, or call 609-720-6740. If you are on active duty in the military, you can get further information about the exams from the DANTES Web site at www.voled.doded.mil/dantes/ exam or e-mail them at exams@voled.doded.mil.

Graduate Record Examination Subject Area Tests. The GRE subject area exams, administered by the Educational Testing Service (ETS), assess knowledge that would ordinarily be acquired during the course of majoring in a subject as an undergraduate. Although they are usually used as entrance exams for graduate schools, some colleges and universities will award undergraduate credit if you get a good score. The subjects include biochemistry, cell and molecular biology; biology; chemistry; computer science; literature in English; mathematics; physics; and psychology.

For more information about the GRE subject area tests, visit the GRE Online site at www.gre.org, send an e-mail to gre-info@ets.org, or call 609-771-7670.

Earning Credits for Life Experience

Many undergraduate degree programs, especially those designed for adults, give credit for knowledge and skills you've gained through life experience. Although the knowledge usually comes through paid employment, it can also be acquired through volunteer work, company or military training courses, travel, recreational activities and hobbies, and reading.

There is a catch, of course—you must document the specifics of what you have learned. It's simply not enough to say that you learned about marketing while selling widgets for XYZ Company. Instead, you must demonstrate what you have learned about pricing, promotion, and product mix; for example, showing plans for a marketing campaign. Thus, to earn credit for life experience, you should assemble a file, or portfolio, of information about your work and other accomplishments. The file may include writing samples, awards, taped presentations or performances, copies of speeches, newspaper articles, official job descriptions, military records, works of art, designs, blueprints, films, or photographs. Your portfolio is then evaluated by an institution's faculty. A student can earn as many as 30 credits—one quarter the number needed for a bachelor's degree—as the result of a good portfolio review. For example, through a portfolio evaluation, a senior marketing executive in her forties earned 30 credits, mostly in marketing and communications, toward her distance learning bachelor's degree from University of Maryland University College. For more information about assessment opportunities for adult learners, check the Web site of the Council for Adult and Experiential Learning (CAEL) at www.cael.org or call 312-499-2600.

Credit for Work Training. Since 1974, thousands of employees have been earning college credit for selected educational programs sponsored by businesses, industry, professional associations, labor unions, and government agencies. The American Council on Education's College Credit Recommendation Service evaluates such programs

> You may be able to earn credits by showing evidence of your knowledge and accomplishments in a portfolio of your work.

according to established college-level criteria and recommends college credit for those programs that measure up to these standards. You can check their Web site at www.acenet.edu, e-mail them at credit@ace.nche.edu, or call 202-939-9475.

Credit for Military Training. Service in the military, specialized training, and occupational experience have the potential to earn you college credit. Many military programs have already been evaluated in terms of their equivalency to college credit. The institutions that belong to Servicemembers Opportunities Colleges (SOC) have agreed to assess students' prior learning and accept each other's credits in transfer. To find out more, check the SOC Web site at www.soc.aascu.org, e-mail them at socmail@aascu.org, or call 800-368-5622 (toll-free).

GRADUATE DEGREE PROGRAMS

Master's Degree

The master's degree is the first academic or professional degree earned after the bachelor's degree. A traditional, full-time master's degree student may take a year or two to earn the required 30 credits. Part-time students usually take longer, it depends on the design of the degree program. In some master's degree programs, students are simply expected to take advanced-level courses and perhaps pass a culminating exam. In others, original research and a thesis are also required. Some distance learning master's degree programs have a brief residency requirement. Students usually earn a Master of Arts (M.A.), a Master of Science (M.S.), or a Master of Business Administration (M.B.A.) degree.

At the time this book was published, distance learning master's degree programs outnumbered other distance learning degree programs by a considerable margin. Most of these degree programs are professional in nature and are designed for working adults with experience in the field. If you are interested in a master's degree in library science, business, or education, you are in luck. These are fields in which there are many distance master's degree programs from which to choose.

Most distance learning doctoral programs, even those offered by virtual universities, have a brief residency requirement.

However, if you are looking for a distance learning master's degree program in an academic field, such as English language and literature, chemistry, or ethnic and cultural studies, your choices are far more limited. That's because most master's programs in academic fields are campus based. Still, *Peterson's Guide to Distance Learning Programs* lists at least one distance master's degree program in each of these academic subject areas.

Another type of master's degree that is offered via distance learning is the interdisciplinary degree. Some are offered in liberal studies or humanities and are granted for advanced study and a culminating project or thesis. Others combine academic and professional areas of study. Still others are offered in broad subject areas like environmental studies, in which students are expected to design their own course of study based on their particular interests.

In the future, the number of distance academic and interdisciplinary master's degree programs is likely to increase, but far slower than the number of professional degree programs, for which the demand is much greater.

Doctoral Degree

The doctoral degree, the highest degree awarded, is earned after an advanced course of study that usually culminates in original research and a dissertation, an extended written work. The traditional on-campus doctoral student takes four to ten years to complete the degree, but many distance learning doctoral programs are structured to streamline the process. Thus, some doctoral degrees can be earned in as little as three years. Most distance learning doctoral programs, even those offered by virtual universities like the University of Phoenix Online, have a brief residency requirement. The Doctor of Philosophy (Ph.D.) is the most common doctoral degree; it is awarded in fields that range from philosophy to geology to communication. Other frequently awarded doctoral degrees include the Doctor of Education (Ed.D.), Doctor of Business Administration (D.B.A.), Doctor of Engineering (Eng.D.), and Doctor of Psychology (Psy.D.). There are far fewer distance learning doctoral programs than master's programs. However, you can find programs in a wide range of fields, although the number of programs within each field may be limited. You can earn a distance learning doctoral degree in fields as diverse as business, engineering, computer science, counseling psychology, instructional technology, education, human services, library science, English literature, management, pharmacy, and public policy. As with distance learning master's degrees, distance learning doctoral degrees tend to be professional rather than academic in orientation. Many of these degree programs are designed with the professional working adult in mind.

Earning Graduate-Level Credit for Knowledge and Experience

There is disagreement among institutions of higher education about whether or not to award graduate-level credit for knowledge acquired outside academia. At present, many graduate schools do not offer credit to students for knowledge and experience acquired before enrollment in the program, no matter how deep or extensive that knowledge and experience may be. However, other less conservative institutions are more open to granting graduate credit for life experience. Check with the schools and programs in which you are interested to see what their policies are.

CERTIFICATE PROGRAMS

Distance learning certificate programs can train you for a new career or give you a foundation in a new subject even if you've already earned a college degree in an entirely different field. A certificate program usually consists of around six to ten courses, all focused on a single profession or subject, and it can be earned at the undergraduate or graduate level. Some schools now offer a portion of a master's or other degree as a certificate. This allows you to take part of the full degree curriculum and either stop at the certification level or proceed through for the entire degree. If this is an option that interests you, be sure to consider the admissions requirements carefully. If you think you may matriculate through to the entire degree, be sure you understand the admissions requirements for each program because they may differ.

Distance learning certificate programs can train you for a new career or give you a foundation in a new subject even if you've already earned a college degree in an entirely different field.

Professional Certificate Programs

To give you just a few examples of professional certificate programs offered via distance learning, within the engineering profession there are certificates in computer-integrated manufacturing, systems engineering, and fire-protection engineering. In business, there are distance learning certificate programs in information technology and health services management. In education, distance learning certificates include early reading instruction, children's literature, and English as a second language. In health care, certificates include medical assisting, home health nursing, and health-care administration. In law, distance learning certificates are offered in paralegal/legal assistant studies and legal issues for business professionals.

Professional certificate programs are often designed with the help of professional associations and licensing boards, and thus encompass real-world, practical knowledge. Many are designed to prepare students for professional certification or licensure. At the end of the program, the student sits for an exam and earns a state-recognized certificate from a certifying agency or licensing board. *If this is your goal, you should make sure that the certification program you want to take meets the certifying agency or licensing board's requirements.* That way, you won't waste your time or money completing a program that won't help you meet your ultimate professional goals.

Certificate Programs in Academic Subjects

Less common, but still available via distance learning, are undergraduate and graduate certificate programs in many academic subjects. At the undergraduate level, you can earn a certificate in areas such as American studies, Chinese language and literature, English composition, creative writing, ethnic and cultural studies, general studies, humanities, and liberal arts and sciences. If you later enroll in an undergraduate degree program, you may be able to apply the credits earned in a certificate program toward your degree.

At the graduate level, you can earn a certificate via distance learning in subjects like biology, English language and literature, geography, physiological psychology, religious studies, and statistics.

INDIVIDUAL COURSES

If you are seeking to update your professional skills, acquire specialized knowledge, earn a few credits toward a degree, or simply take a class for your own pleasure, individual distance learning courses may be for you. Many institutions of higher education venture into distance learning by offering a few classes scattered throughout various departments. As their experience with distance education increases, they begin to offer complete programs of study. Thus, if you are interested in just taking a few courses, you have the widest range of choices. You can find individual courses in subjects that range from accounting to animal sciences and from art history to aviation—and that's just a random sample beginning with the letter *A*.

There are several options that may be open to you when you take an individual course, such as taking the course for credit, taking it without earning credit, or earning Continuing Education Units (CEUs). The option you select depends on your purpose for taking the course.

Taking a Course for Credit

If you are enrolled in a degree program and need a few credits, taking a distance learning course may help you satisfy your degree requirements. Your own college or university may offer courses via distance learning. In fact, students enrolled in conventional on-campus degree programs sometimes take distance learning courses from their schools when they go home for the summer. For example, Iowa's Drake University offers online summer courses to its students.

If your own institution does not offer suitable distance learning courses, you may be able to take a distance education course from any regionally accredited college or university and get credit for it. You may even be able to save some tuition money if you select a course at a community college or a less expensive four-year college or university. The credits you earn will probably be transferable to the institution in which you are enrolled. *But before you enroll in a course at another college or university, be sure to check with your own school to make sure it will accept the credits.* Many colleges and universities require that you obtain a minimum number of credits from core courses and courses in your

Before you enroll in a distance learning course from another college or university, be sure to check with your own school to make sure it will accept the credits.

major in order to earn their degree. To avoid losing time and money on a course that won't be recognized by your school, it's wise to check with your academic adviser and work out a degree plan before you take courses from other institutions. If you are not currently enrolled in a degree program but think you may be in the future, taking a couple of distance education courses for credit is a good way to see whether or not a distance education degree program is for you. Later you may be able to apply the credits toward your degree.

Noncredit Courses

If learning for the sake of learning or acquiring specific professional knowledge is your goal, taking a distance education course on a noncredit basis may be the way to go. Such courses may help you prepare for a new career or study for professional licensure and certification.

Just as you can audit an on-campus course for a lesser charge than if you were taking the course for credit, you can audit a distance learning course as well. Students who audit a course don't receive a grade, so they are not usually required to turn in assignments or take exams. Still, many do so in order to maximize the learning experience.

Continuing Education Units

Distance learning is a good option if your profession requires continuing education, even after you've earned your degree, certificate, or license.

Distance learning is a good option for working adults whose professions require continuing education, even after they've earned their degree, certificate, or license. Many states mandate continuing education for people in professions such as teaching, nursing, and accounting. For example, New Jersey requires teachers to complete 100 hours of professional development work every five years. Professionals in engineering, business, and computer science may also opt to keep up with developments in their field through distance learning. If you take a distance learning course for professional enhancement, you don't necessarily have to earn regular college credits for it. Instead, you may be able to earn Continuing Education Units. The CEU system is a nationally recognized program that provides a standardized measure for accumulating, transferring, and recognizing participation in continuing education programs. One CEU is defined as 10 contact hours of participation in an organized continuing education experience under responsible sponsorship, capable direction, and qualified instruction. Some institutions will permit you to take courses for continuing education credits rather than for regular credit or no credit. It is still important to take the courses from a properly accredited program, however, so that employers and professional agencies will recognize them.

FINDING PROGRAMS AND COURSES

The Internet

The Internet is an excellent place to start your search for information about distance learning courses and programs. Perhaps the most comprehensive database of distance learning offerings is the one maintained by Peterson's at www.petersons.com/dlearn. Peterson's, an education information provider and publisher of college directories and other education-related material (including this book), provides online access to current information about distance learning programs and courses. You can search the Peterson's distance learning database in a number of ways: by institution, degree program, or field of study. Once you have found courses or programs that match your search criteria, there are links to further information about them. Peterson's distance learning database is especially good for locating degree programs, including undergraduate and graduate certificates, associate's degrees, bachelor's degrees, master's degrees, and doctoral degrees.

Another Internet database is the International Distance Learning Course Finder, provided by International Where and How. When you search for a course, you can specify course subject, course name, country, or institution; and you can narrow the search by language of instruction, mode of instructional technology, and type of credit you are seeking. The Course Finder seemed to work well for locating individual courses, but it seemed less efficient when asked to locate degree programs.

If you have particular institutions in mind, you can log on to their Web sites to find out about their distance learning courses and degrees. Some of these sites provide distance learning self-assessments and explanations of course delivery systems as well as academic information about courses and programs.

Print Directories

Print directories are another excellent source of information about distance education courses and degree programs. *Peterson's Guide to Distance Learning Programs* is the most comprehensive directory, it covers nearly 3,000 degree and certificate programs at more than 1,000 colleges and universities and offers even more information than the online database. In the directory, institutions that offer distance learning courses and degree programs are listed alphabetically and their offerings are briefly described. The directory has several indexes that make it easy to locate specific information. You can search the indexes for subject area degree programs, courses in specific fields of study, and geographic location. If you are interested in distance education programs in Canada, you can consult the *Guide to Distance Learning Programs in Canada*, published by Education International.

A word of caution about using the print directories: There are many directories still in libraries and bookstores that were published just a year or two ago but that are already quite out of date. So many new distance learning courses and degree programs are being offered each year that you must make sure you consult the most recent directories. Otherwise, you may miss the ideal course or program for you.

Who Offers Distance Education?

Chapter 4

As communication technologies have improved and the need for continuous lifelong learning has increased, the nature of postsecondary education has begun to change. Traditional colleges and universities, which used to be the sole purveyors of higher education, now find themselves competing with a range of unconventional providers, including corporate universities, for-profit virtual universities, and unaffiliated distance learning providers. From the student's point of view, the array of institutions that offer distance learning can be confusing. What difference does it make to you whether you take a distance learning course or program from a traditional college, through a consortium of institutions of higher education, from one of the new virtual universities, or from an unaffiliated online provider?

Whether or not the institution matters depends on your purpose. If you just take a few courses for professional development or for your own pleasure and never plan to seek certification or college credit, then your choice of institution is not critical. You can just choose the distance learning provider that seems to have the courses that best suit your informal needs. However, if you plan to earn college credit, professional certification, or a degree, your choice of provider becomes much more important. You must choose an institution whose courses and degrees are widely recognized and accepted in your field. That may mean sticking to the accredited bricks-and-mortar colleges for distance learning programs, or it may mean enrolling in an innovative degree program from a virtual university only a few years old. In this chapter, we'll describe some of the institutions and partnerships that offer distance learning in order to acquaint you with the variety of providers that exists. In the next chapter, we will explain some criteria that you can use to evaluate distance education offerings.

TRADITIONAL COLLEGES AND UNIVERSITIES

The most familiar group of distance education providers consists of the traditional colleges, universities, graduate schools, community colleges, technical schools, and vocational schools. In these institutions, distance education arose as individual administrators and faculty members took the initiative to use new technologies to deliver off-campus instruction to students. As the number of courses grew, many institutions developed whole degree programs as the next step.

Among the traditional colleges and universities, public institutions are more likely to offer distance education courses and degree programs than private institutions. In addition, larger institutions are more likely to have distance learning offerings than smaller institutions.

Traditional colleges and universities enter the distance learning market with solid educational credentials.

The greatest advantage that most traditional colleges and universities bring to the distance education field is that they are established, well-known institutions with reputable faculty members and lots of experience in education. In other words, they enter the distance learning market with solid educational credentials. If they fall short, it is likely to be in the areas of instructional and information technology. Because a lot of distance education courses are developed ad hoc, the quality of the instructional technology may vary considerably, even from one course to another within the same school. In addition, traditional colleges and universities may fall short in information technology support for faculty members and students. For example, the Gartner Group, an information technology research organization, recommends that organizations have one information technology staff person for every 50 to 75 users. In contrast, colleges and universities report an average of one technical support person for every 150 to 800 users. Recognizing this shortcoming, many colleges and universities have established policies and procedures to set up instructional technology standards and consistency, and they have increased their technical resources and training efforts to support faculty members and students. In addition, because developing quality distance education courses and programs is time-consuming and expensive, colleges and universities have begun to form partnerships to pool their resources. These partnerships, called consortia, have quickly developed into major players in the world of distance higher education.

CONSORTIA

Distance learning consortia are associations or partnerships of higher education institutions that have agreed to cooperate to provide distance learning courses and resources. Most consortia are designed to provide students with a greater selection of both courses and faculty expertise than is available at a single institution. Some consortia also offer centralized student and faculty support services. Just as there are many variations on the basic on-campus program, there are many distance education consortium models too.

It's important to remember that most distance learning consortia are not degree-granting institutions to which the student applies. Though there are exceptions to this, as in the case of Western Governors University and National Technological University (discussed later in the chapter), students normally apply directly to at least one school in the consortium as a means of accessing the resources of other member institutions.

Almost without exception, accredited universities in consortia have roughly the same application procedures and admissions requirements for distance degree programs as for traditional campus-based programs. In general, minimum grade point averages, standardized test scores of a certain percentile, and letters of recommendation or intent are required for both bachelor's and master's degree programs. The exception is the competency-based program that waives academic credentials and previous schooling and instead uses workplace experience and learned skill-based assessments to place students. So why do you need to know about consortia if you probably will never apply to one? The answer is that by enrolling in a college or university degree program, you may find yourself in a consortium without even realizing it, especially if you attend a state university.

By enrolling at a traditional college or university, you may find yourself in a consortium without even realizing it.

Types of Consortia

Over the last few years, several types of consortia have emerged as the most successful and most popular distance education models. Among them are statewide consortia of public universities and colleges, statewide consortia of public and private institutions, regional consortia, consortia of peer institutions of higher education, and specialized consortia.

Statewide Consortia of Public Colleges and Universities. On the tightly focused side of the spectrum, a consortium may consist of the campuses of a single state university system. Students access the distance learning offerings of the various state colleges through a portal sometimes referred to as a virtual university.

> **Some consortia offer a centralized system of student services as well as serve as a portal to courses from member institutions.**

A good example of a public statewide consortium is the University of Texas TeleCampus collaboration, which consists of fifteen UT campuses (www.telecampus.utsystem.edu). In collaborative degree plans offered via the TeleCampus, you may apply to one school, take courses from several partner institutions, use centralized support services, and receive a fully accredited degree from the "home" campus to which you originally applied. The TeleCampus serves as both a portal to distance education offerings in the Texas system and as a centralized point of service.

Many other states operate or develop consortia of their public colleges and universities, including Connecticut, Illinois, Kansas, Massachusetts, Michigan, New Jersey, New York, Ohio, Oklahoma, Oregon, South Dakota, and Tennessee. All have arrangements in place whereby students can take some transferable credits on line from more than one institution and apply them to a degree at their home institution.

Statewide Consortia of Public and Private Colleges and Universities. Broadening the scope a bit is the statewide consortium that includes both public and private institutions of higher education. Students in the state can use a single Web site to select distance education courses offered by member colleges and universities. If you are enrolled in a degree program at one member institution, you have access to distance learning courses given by other member institutions. Although the consortia members typically work together to maximize the transferability of credits from one college or university to another, it is still usually up to you to ensure that credits earned elsewhere can be applied to your home institution's degree.

For example, Kentucky Commonwealth Virtual University (KCVU) encompasses more than fifty institutions in the state of Kentucky, ranging from universities to technical colleges (www.kcvu.org). Each member institution charges its own tuition rates for in-state and out-of-state students. In addition to maintaining a centralized Internet directory of all distance learning courses offered in Kentucky, KCVU offers exceptional student support services. For example, you can fill out a common form to apply on line to any of the fifty member institutions. Once you are admitted to the KCVU system, you have centralized online access to every library book in the system as well as online access to the full text of 5,000 journals. If you wish to check out a book, it will be sent to the nearest public library, where you can pick it up free of charge. If there is no library nearby, the book will be sent by courier to your home or office. Your academic records will be maintained by each institution at which you take a course, but also by KCVU, which will keep your complete records from all institutions.

Regional Consortia. Regional consortia include institutions of higher education from more than one state. Such consortia may involve public institutions, private institutions, or a mix of both. The Southern Regional Education Board (SREB) launched the Southern Regional Electronic Campus (SREC) in 1998 and now offers more than 3,200 courses from 262 colleges and universities in sixteen states (www. electroniccampus.org). SREC attempts to guarantee a standard of quality in the courses it lists by reviewing them to make sure they are well set up and supported by adequate services. It does not judge curriculum (it leaves that to member institutions) nor does it list courses in their first year of instruction.

From the Electronic Campus Web site, you can identify distance learning programs and courses that are available from all member institutions. For more detailed information, you can search the site by college or university, discipline, level, and state, including course descriptions and how the programs and courses are delivered. You can also connect directly to a particular college or university to learn about registration, enrollment, and cost. To improve its student services, the Electronic Campus has formed a partnership with the University System of Georgia to create a new Web site known as Ways In (www.waysin.org). From that site, due to be operational in 2001–02, students will be able to apply for admission, register for classes, get information about and apply for financial aid, make payments, purchase textbooks, and use new online library services.

The SREC system is administratively decentralized. The acceptance of transfer credits and the use of credits for program requirements are determined by the college or university in which the student is enrolled. Likewise, all institutions set their own levels for in-state and out-of-state tuition, maintain individual student records, and determine policy with respect to access to their own student services. Therefore, if you take three classes from three different institutions you might have to be admitted to all three, pay three different tuition rates, and contact all three institutions for your academic records. A unique model of regional distance education collaboration, consisting of members from nineteen states, is Western Governors University (www.wgu.edu). Unlike most other virtual universities that serve as the hub of a consortium, WGU enrolls its own students and grants its own degrees by assessing students' knowledge through competency-based examinations. WGU does not teach its own courses, but it provides its students with access to courses from member institutions. WGU, established in 1998, is not yet regionally accredited, although it was awarded candidacy status in 2000 and hopes to be fully accredited in two to five years (see Chapter 5 for more on accreditation). Its unusual degree model and accreditation status may account for WGU's relatively low enrollment of about 200 degree-seeking students.

Other regional consortia include the National Universities Degree Consortium, a collaboration of ten accredited universities from across the United States (www.nudc.org); and the Canadian Virtual University, which includes seven universities across Canada (www.cvu-uvc.ca). Today, students can even choose to participate in a global consortium like CREAD, the Inter-American network of institutions throughout North, Central, and South America.

If you take three classes from three different institutions in a highly decentralized consortium, you might have to be admitted to all three, pay three different tuition rates, and contact all three institutions for your academic records.

Consortia of Peer Institutions of Higher Education. Groups of institutions sometimes form consortia because they have a common orientation or complementary strengths from which students might benefit.

For example, the Jesuit Distance Education Network of the Association of Jesuit Colleges and Universities seeks to expand the array of learning options for students on its twenty-four campuses in nineteen states (www.jesuitnet.com). Administrators hope to develop the JesuitNET system so that a student enrolled at any member institution will be able to take fully transferable online courses at any other member institution. Tuition rates will be set by individual colleges and universities. Through its Web site, JesuitNET promotes these schools' online degree and certificate programs as well as individual courses.

Another, more recent private college and university consortium uses a "team teaching" approach to deliver courses to students on multiple campuses. Thirteen institutions in the Associated Colleges of the South have created a "virtual classics department," (www.sunoikisis. org). In this case, students must all log on at the same time in order to tune in to an online audio broadcast of a lecture. During the lecture students may pose questions and make comments in a live chat room. Classes are "team taught" in the sense that professors from several campuses may take responsibility for course material and all log on together with the students.

Specialized Consortia. Some consortia are formed by institutions that focus on a particular field. For example, National Technological University (NTU) is one of the oldest technology-based consortia (www. ntu.edu). A global university, NTU, arranges for its member colleges and universities across the country to deliver advanced technical education and training, usually to employees of corporate clients. Currently, more than 1,200 courses are available through NTU's participating universities, which provides fourteen master's degree programs. An unusual aspect of the NTU consortium is that the consortium itself, rather than the member institutions, is the degree-granting body.

NTU's focus is on technical education and training that is ready to use in the workforce. Its corporate customers typically have purchased the equipment necessary to receive the courses. Though students who are not employed by an NTU corporate client may take courses, they must pay an extra fee to have tapes or CD-ROMs of courses sent to them. NTU has also partnered with the Public Broadcasting System (PBS) to create the Business and Technology Network, a series of more than seventy-five engineering programs per year delivered directly to organizations via satellite.

Pros and Cons of Consortia Learning Models

One obvious advantage of consortia is the pooling of resources. More university partners translates to more choices in curriculum, and often a shared expense in developing instructional design and technology. Consortia can offer a centralized database or course schedule that allows you to find members' courses easily rather than having to search many institutions' materials and Web sites for what you need. You may also have the chance to choose from among a group of respected faculty members from within the consortia, which allows you to find the teachers with expertise most closely suited to your academic and professional interests. This large sampling of faculty members tends to offer a more diverse worldview in the classroom. And, a consortium can often provide essential student services on a scale not fiscally achievable by a single university. For example, a dozen universities can pool resources for a much broader digital library than any single school could supply on its own.

However, from the student's point of view, consortia can have problems, many of which can be attributed to their relative newness. The most critical of these for students are problems with transferring credits. Other drawbacks may include large class sizes and problems in communication.

Problems with Transferring Credits. One problem that sometimes comes up for students trying to earn an entire degree, or part of a degree, on line is that their home institution may require a minimum number of "home" credits, yet it may not offer enough courses via distance learning for a student to meet that minimum. "I am concerned because [my home campus] offers a limited number of online classes," says Andrea Bessel, who is working toward a bachelor's degree in business administration with a concentration in finance. Bessel, who works full time and prefers the convenience of online to on-campus courses, has been taking classes from several institutions in the State University of New York (SUNY) Learning Network (www.sln.suny. edu). "It is great that other SUNY campuses offer more courses," continues Bessel, "but I am concerned about accumulating too many transfer credits—you are only allowed so many."

In the future, this problem is likely to arise less often for several reasons. First, as distance education degree programs become more common and well known, students are likely to search them out and apply directly to the institution that offers them. In contrast, like many other students, Bessel applied to her local state college campus and only later discovered that taking online courses within the statewide system was much more convenient than traveling to class. Second, individual institutions will continue to add to their distance education offerings, broadening the course choices for their "home" students. And third, some state systems and other consortia may eventually decide to liberalize their rules on transfer credit maximums within the consortium as the demand for distance degrees increases.

Indeed, some consortia have already succeeded in solving credit transfer problems, and others are addressing the challenge of reconciling differing credit transfer policies and logistics. *However, to ensure that any courses you take will successfully transfer from one institution to another (and ultimately toward your degree), you should secure an academic adviser at the start of your program and investigate the transferrability of credits before you register for courses at other institutions within the consortium.* Serving as your own adviser brings the risk that some courses may ultimately not transfer toward your degree.

Large Class Size. Because so many students have access to courses in a consortium, online classes may reach an unmanageable size if limits are not placed on the student-to-teacher ratio. Many schools now adopt a ceiling on the number of students allowed in an online class, with teaching assistants or subsections of the course added for each

To avoid credit transfer problems, consult your academic adviser and ascertain that credits will be transferrable *before* you enroll in courses at other institutions in the consortium.

additional set of students. This is vital to the processing of information and interaction required in the successful online course. Faculty members often find that a class of 25 students is quite manageable, but more may become problematic.

Miscommunication. Communication may be difficult in a consortium. The larger the consortium, the more likely that many universities or university systems are involved, and therefore you may need to communicate with several institutions that have differing policies and procedures. Additional communication snags can arise when you try to move your student records from one campus to the next. Some consortia have spent considerable time, effort, and money to make this tedious and laborious process appear seamless to you as a student. For those that have not, you should be prepared to take a proactive stance in helping to see that your records are successfully moved from one department, college, or university to another.

> In today's workplace and economy, many students opt for the flexibility and increased curriculum choices of a consortium over an individual school.

COMPARING THE SINGLE UNIVERSITY TO THE CONSORTIUM

A student who is looking for a learning community with school pride and a great deal of local loyalty may find the multicampus environment of a consortium less desirable than the collegiality of the single university environment. In today's workplace and economy, however, many students opt for the flexibility and increased curriculum choices of a consortium over an individual school. Many consortia have succeeded in creating a sense of community for learners, and many more are attempting to do so. The high level of dialogue in the online environment can often build friendships, connections, and communities not achieved in a traditional environment. A single university can offer you the chance to immerse yourself in one department (of your major, for example), but a consortium can offer a wider variety of choices in mentors and philosophies. As a student, you should think about which you'd prefer.

VIRTUAL UNIVERSITIES

In recent years, the development of communication technology has led to a new type of institution called a virtual university. It's a school without a campus that delivers instruction and degree programs exclusively via technology and usually for a profit. The University of Phoenix Online, Walden University, the United States Open University, and Jones International University are all examples of virtual universities. Some of these institutions have years of experience in distance learning and have evolved as the technologies have changed. For example, Walden University is more than thirty years old, and the University of Phoenix Online was established in 1989 as an offshoot of the University of Phoenix, which was founded in 1976. Others, like the United States Open University, are newly established with a much shorter track record. What most of these institutions have in common is a focus on education for adults. Their course offerings, degree programs, and student services are all geared toward the busy working adult who needs the flexibility of distance education. For example, courses at the University of Phoenix Online are delivered via the Internet. Students take one 5-week course at a time, which allows them to focus their effort intensively on one subject. Student services can be accessed via the university Web site. "We are customer-service oriented," says Russell Paden, regional executive director of academic affairs at the University of Phoenix Online. "We make things easy and convenient for the student." Virtual universities have a mixed reputation in the world of higher education. Although their degrees are accepted by many employers, they are often looked down upon by traditional academics. A few are regionally accredited, some are too new to be accredited, and some are modern versions of the old diploma mills (see Chapter 5 for more on accreditation).

For-profit virtual universities that teach entirely at a distance tailor their degree programs, instructional design, and student services for adult learners.

From a student's point of view, then, the biggest disadvantage of a virtual university may be its less-than-stellar educational reputation, whether deserved or not. A great advantage of the best of these institutions, however, is that they tend to be sophisticated in terms of instructional technology and design and technical support. To the student, this can mean ease, convenience, and flexibility.

THE NEW ONLINE PROVIDERS

The growth of the distance learning market in higher education, continuing education, and training has attracted investors and educators who are eager to provide courses to adults, primarily via the Internet. There are many of these startup ventures, and they take many forms. A few examples to illustrate:

- UNext.com is working with faculty members from prestigious schools like Columbia and Stanford to develop online business courses for the corporate market. At present, it is piloting courses with groups of employees from large corporations. Eventually it hopes to offer a complete M.B.A. program as well as other degrees through its subsidiary, Cardean University.
- The Global Education Network (GEN) plans to offer distance education courses from some of the top colleges in the United States, including Brown, Wellesley, and Williams.
- Harcourt General Inc., a publisher, has established Harcourt Higher Education, an online college.
- KaplanCollege.com is planning to offer graduate courses for teachers through the John F. Kennedy University.

All of these ventures are so new that it's impossible to guess which will still exist in five years' time. In the next few years, the new online providers will begin to sort themselves out as some models succeed and some fail. If you are taking courses through your employer or for personal reasons, you may find that one of these companies has courses that meet your needs. If, however, you are looking for a degree program, you are better off sticking with well-established institutions of higher education, at least at present.

Selecting a Good Distance Learning Program

Chapter 5

As a prospective distance learning student, you should begin to evaluate programs in which you are interested as much as you would any campus-based, traditional program. The first question, of course, is: Does the curriculum meet your educational and professional goals? If it doesn't, there's not much point in looking into that program any further, however flexible and convenient it seems. If the program does seem to meet your educational needs, then the real work of evaluating it must begin.

Distance education students need to be especially concerned about the quality of the programs they are considering for two main reasons. First, there are a lot of diploma mills out there. As we've seen, there has been a proliferation of distance learning degree programs spurred by the Internet. Many are legitimate, but some are not. As one distance bachelor's degree student put it, "Admission to some online programs consists of nothing more than your name, date of birth, and a check." In fact, to demonstrate how easy it is to set up an online "university" that looks authentic, Emir Mohammed created a Web site for Oxford Open University, a fictitious virtual university, complete with a list of imaginary faculty members with degrees from bogus institutions. So if you run across a school that promises you a degree for little time, effort, or money, be cautious. If it sounds too good to be true, it probably is.

The second reason distance learning students must be especially careful about quality is that in many quarters, distance degrees are still considered the poor relations of degrees earned on campus. "One area of confusion for working adult students is the reaction to distance learning from traditional academia," says Russell Paden, regional

www.petersons.com   *Game Plan for Distance Learning*   **69** executive director of academic affairs for the University of Phoenix Online. "Although attitudes are changing, some in the traditional academic world still think their way is the only way." Robert V. Steiner, who directs the distance learning project at Teachers College, Columbia University, agrees. "For better or worse, justly or not," he says, "there continues to be a perception that distance education degree programs are inferior to traditional programs." Fritz J. Messere, associate professor of broadcasting at the State University of New York at Oswego, thinks that in five or six years, that attitude will change. "When we see what the people with distance degrees actually accomplish in the future, our reluctance to acknowledge that these are real degrees and meaningful educational experiences will disappear."

However, in the meantime you need to evaluate each distance education program that looks promising to ensure that its certificate or degree will be of value to you in the future. What can you do to ensure that a distance credential will be recognized in the academic, professional, and/or business communities? What can you do to assess whether or not the program and the university are of high quality? Basically, you must do a lot of research. You must gather information from the program, university, accrediting agencies, professional associations, faculty, current and former students, and colleagues. Only then can you make an informed decision about whether a program is good as well as right for you.

To guide you in this task, this chapter describes some of the criteria you should keep in mind as you evaluate each distance education program. *Pay particular attention to the sections on reputation and accreditation.* More than any other factors, a school and program's reputation and accreditation status can serve as benchmarks of quality that will affect the value of your degree.

REPUTATION

"Look for a brand name—a recognized university," suggests Fritz J. Messere of SUNY Oswego. For many students, the reputation of the school is the paramount factor in selecting a program. Sonja Cole, a middle-school media specialist who is enrolled in a continuing professional education program at Rutgers University in New Jersey, explains, "I know that Rutgers has an excellent reputation for academic rigor, so I assumed that their online courses would be just as challenging and stimulating." She continues, "The most important factor to me was the reputation of the school, because distance learning programs are not always taken seriously by administrators and business people . . . If you can say you took distance courses at a very reputable school, they will be more likely to give you credit." Not only should you consider the reputation of a university in general, you should consider the reputation of a distance degree from a university *in your field*. For example, if you plan to earn a bachelor's degree at a distance to prepare for graduate work, find out whether or not graduate programs in your field will accept an undergraduate distance degree, even from a reputable institution.

"If you are in doubt about the validity of a distance degree in your chosen field, ask around," advises Patti Wolf, assistant professor of computer science at University of Maryland University College. When Wolf was looking for a doctoral program for herself, almost all of her colleagues advised her that a distance degree would not be as well accepted in her chosen career as a traditional degree. Another doctoral student, who is earning an Ed.D. from a relatively new virtual university, regrets that "the one thing I didn't do [was] speak to administrators in local universities to review the reputation of the school I finally chose. Even though the program is still exactly what I wanted and the convenience, schedule, and costs meet my needs, the public perception of this program is not wonderful." Carla Gentry, who is earning a distance master's degree in nursing (nurse practitioner) at Gonzaga University in Washington, puts the importance of reputation succinctly: "You wouldn't want to spend all that time and money and then find out that the degree isn't worth anything."

ACCREDITATION

The accreditation status of a college, university, or program can give you an indication of its general quality and reputation. But just what does accreditation mean, and how does it affect distance learners?

> **"The most important factor to me was the reputation of the school, because distance learning programs are not always taken seriously by administrators and business people."**

> **"If you are in doubt about the validity of a distance degree in your chosen field, ask around."**

What Is Accreditation?

In the United States, authority over postsecondary educational institutions is decentralized. The states, not the federal government, have the authority to regulate educational institutions within their borders, and as a consequence, standards and quality vary considerably for "state-approved" schools. You will find many state-approved schools that are not accredited, and many that are.

In order to ensure a basic level of quality, the practice of accrediting institutions arose. Private, nongovernmental educational agencies with a regional or national scope have adopted standards to evaluate whether or not colleges and universities provide educational programs at basic levels of quality. Institutions that seek accreditation conduct an in-depth self-study to measure their performance against the standards. The accrediting agency then conducts an on-site evaluation and either awards accreditation or preaccreditation status—or denies accreditation. Periodically the agency reevaluates each institution to make sure its continued accreditation is warranted. So accreditation is not a one-shot deal—an institution must maintain high standards or it runs the risk of jeopardizing its accreditation status as a result of one of the periodic evaluations.

Seeking accreditation is entirely voluntary on the part of the institution of higher education. The initial accreditation process takes a long time—as much as five or ten years—and it costs money. You can see that a very new school will not have been in operation long enough to be accredited. We gave an example of this in the last chapter: Western Governors University, a virtual university established in 1998, was awarded accreditation *candidacy* status in 2000 and, if all goes well, will be fully accredited in two to five years. Of course, being awarded candidacy status does not ensure that an institution will eventually be fully accredited.

Institutional and Specialized Accreditation

There are two basic types of accreditation: institutional accreditation and specialized accreditation. Institutional accreditation is awarded to an institution by one of six regional accrediting agencies and many national accrediting agencies, such as the Distance Education and Training Council. The regional accrediting agencies play the largest role in institutional accreditation (see the Appendix for a list of the regional accrediting agencies). If a college or university is regionally accredited, that means that the institution as a whole has met the accrediting agency's standards. Within the institution, particular programs and departments contribute to the institution's objectives at varying levels of quality. There are several benefits of enrolling in a program at a regionally accredited college or university:

- You are assured of a basic level of quality education and services.
- Any credits you earn are more likely to be transferable to other regionally accredited institutions, although we've seen that each institution makes its own decisions on transfer credits on a case-by-case basis.
- Any certificate or degree you earn is more likely to be recognized by other colleges and universities and by employers as a legitimate credential.
- You may qualify for federal loans and grants because regionally accredited institutions are eligible to participate in Title IV financial aid programs (see Chapter 8 for more on financial aid).

In contrast to institutional accreditation, specialized accreditation usually applies to a single department, program, or school that is part of a larger institution of higher education. The accredited unit may be as big as a college within a university or as small as a curriculum within a field of study. Most specialized accrediting agencies review units within institutions that are regionally accredited, although some also accredit freestanding institutions. There are specialized accrediting agencies in almost fifty fields, including allied health, art and design, Bible college education, business, engineering, law, marriage and family therapy, nursing, psychology, and theology. Specialized accreditation may or may not be a consideration for you when you evaluate distance education programs. That's because the role of specialized accreditation varies considerably depending on the field of study. In some professional fields, you must have a degree or certificate from a

If a college or university is regionally accredited, that means that the institution as a whole has met the accrediting agency's standards.

Specialized accreditation usually applies to a single department, program, or school that is part of a larger institution of higher education.

program with specialized accreditation in order to take qualifying exams or practice the profession. In other fields, specialized accreditation has little or no effect on your ability to work. Thus, it's especially important that you find out what role accreditation plays in your field since it may affect your professional future as well as the quality of your education.

Checking on a School and Its Accreditors

Since accreditation is awarded by private organizations, any group can hang out a shingle and proclaim itself an accrediting agency. Some diploma mills, for example, have been known to create their own accrediting agency and then proclaim themselves "accredited." So how can you tell (1) if the school or college in which you are interested is regionally accredited, (2) if the program has the specialized accreditation you need, and (3) if the agencies that have accredited the school and program are legitimate? Of course, you can simply ask the school or program, but since accreditation is so important, it's probably a lot wiser to check elsewhere.

First, check with the regional accrediting agency that covers the state in which the school is located. Then check with any specialized accrediting agency that may assess the particular program in which you are interested.

To find out if an accrediting agency is legitimate and nationally recognized, you can consult the Council for Higher Education Accreditation (CHEA), a private agency that accredits the accreditors (www.chea.org). Or you can check with the U.S. Department of Education. Their Web site has a complete list of institutional and specialized accrediting agencies recognized by the federal government (www.ed.gov/offices/OPE/accreditation/natlagencies.html). This Web site will also tell you whether or not accreditation by a particular agency makes the school eligible to participate in federal financial aid programs. A list of regional and specialized accrediting agencies, with contact information, is also provided in the Appendix.

> It's important to find out what role accreditation plays in your field since it may affect your professional future as well as the quality of your education.

> Since accreditation is awarded by private organizations, any group can hang out a shingle and proclaim itself an accrediting agency.

Checking on Canadian Institutions of Higher Education

In Canada, as in the United States, there is no centralized governmental accrediting agency. Instead, the provincial governments evaluate the quality of university programs in each province, with a few nationwide agencies evaluating professional programs. To check on a Canadian university, you can contact the appropriate provincial department of education. To get general information about accreditation in Canada, visit the Web site of the Council of Ministers of Education at www. cmec.ca. Their Web site also has contact information and links to the provincial departments of education.

Checking on an Unaccredited Institution

As we've seen, seeking accreditation is a voluntary process, and some legitimate schools choose not to undertake it. In addition, the newer virtual universities may not have been around long enough to be accredited. So what can you do to make sure a school is legitimate if it is not accredited?

First, you can call the state agency with jurisdiction over higher education in the state in which the school is located. The agency can at least tell you whether or not the school is operating with a legitimate charter, and it may be able to tell you if any complaints have been lodged or legal action taken against it. Second, you can call the school and ask why it is not accredited and whether the school has plans to seek accreditation. If the school tells you it has applied for accreditation, double-check its status with the agency it names. Third, you can consult with people in your field about the school's reputation and the value of its degree. Remember, in some fields, a degree from an unaccredited school or program will bar you from professional licensure and practice. So keep in mind that enrolling in an unaccredited school or program can be risky. If you can avoid it, do so.

Accreditation Issues Relating to Distance Education

In the United States during the 1990s, controversy arose over the accreditation of online programs within traditional universities and the accreditation of completely virtual universities. On the one hand, many felt that online degree programs should be evaluated using the same criteria as other degree programs within institutions of higher education. Others thought that new standards were needed to properly evaluate distance education.

Although this issue has not yet been settled, the six regional accrediting agencies have proposed uniform guidelines for evaluating distance education. The impetus for this move is the fact that many distance education programs cross regional borders; the agencies want to ensure that similar standards are adopted across the country. Among the proposed criteria specific to accrediting distance education are faculty control of course content, technical and program support for both faculty members and students, and evaluation and assessment methods for measuring student learning. However, until these or other guidelines are accepted, distance education programs will continue to be evaluated using the same criteria as on-campus programs.

PROGRAM QUALITY

The reputation of a college or university and its accreditation status can give you a broad idea of its standing in the academic and professional world. If you are pursuing a graduate degree or know your field of interest as an undergraduate, it's important to separate the reputation of the program or department in which you are interested from the reputation of the university to which it belongs. Granted, in many cases, both the program and the university will have similar reputations. But in some cases, you may find a below average program at an excellent university or an above average program at a university with a lesser reputation.

Keep in mind that you should be looking for a high-quality curriculum and good faculty; the fact that the program is taught at a distance should be secondary. "I chose this program because it would have been one of my top three choices if I had decided to pursue a full-time [on-campus] master's program," explains Lara Hollenczer, who is earning a distance master's degree in communications management at Syracuse University. Hollenczer suggests talking to professors and current students to get a better idea of a program in which you are interested.

Academic Quality

One way to assess the quality of a program, as we have seen, is to find out whether or not it is accredited by a specialized agency—if that applies in your field. But there are other ways to assess a program's academic quality. First, look at the curriculum. Does it cover what you need to learn? Is the syllabus up to date? For one master's degree student in nursing (family nurse practitioner studies), the quality of the curriculum was the factor that led her to choose Gonzaga University. "I definitely wanted to know that when I graduated I would have a good education and know what I was doing," she explains.

Next, check some of the program's student data. For example, what percentage of students who enroll actually complete the degree? What percentage of students is employed in a field relating to their studies? What are some of the program's graduates doing today? A program with a high completion rate and successful graduates is preferable to one with a high dropout rate.

Faculty

Second, check out the faculty members. What are their credentials? What are their areas of expertise? Are they well-regarded in their field? If the program is professional in nature, look for faculty members with a blend of academic background and professional experience. If the program is academic, you should find out whether tenure-track professors with Ph.D.s teach both the on-campus and distance courses or if distance courses are relegated to part-time adjunct faculty members and/or assistants. Finally, evaluate whether or not the faculty is experienced both with the course content and with the instructional medium. If a program looks interesting to you, get in touch with a couple of

"I chose this program because it would have been one of my top three choices if I had decided to pursue a full-time [on-campus] master's program."

Find out whether the same professors teach the on-campus and distance courses or if distance courses are taught by adjunct faculty members and/or assistants.

faculty members to discuss it. You can tell a lot about a program by whether or not the faculty members are willing to take some time to talk to prospective students.

Experience with Adult Learners

A third area of concern is the program's experience with adult learners. If you're an adult learner and choose to enroll in a college oriented to young undergraduates, you may find yourself struggling to cope. "My concern would be that in some programs the adult learner is an afterthought," says Claudine SchWeber, assistant vice president for distance education and lifelong learning at University of Maryland University College. "Adults are more critical consumers, and that won't fly these days." Working adult students have different needs than full-time on-campus students, and assessing the degree to which a program takes those needs into account can help you decide whether or not a program is a good match for you.

For Robin Barnes, who is pursuing a distance master's degree in nursing (family nurse practitioner studies) at Gonzaga University, the flexibility of the faculty in dealing with adult students was extremely important. "We were adult learners who had lives and jobs outside of school. If we needed more time for a paper due to work schedules or a family crisis, the instructors were very understanding." Carla Gentry, in the same program, agrees. "The most important factor to me is the flexibility of the program and the staff's willingness to work with my schedule."

Instructional Design and Technology

There are several areas that fall under the broad category of instructional design and technology that you should assess for each program you consider.

Is the Instructional Technology a Good Match for the Content?

Your first concern in the area of instructional design and technology should be whether or not the delivery system and the content are a good match. "How can you evaluate whether the technology and content

"The most important factor to me is the flexibility of the program and the staff's willingness to work with my schedule."

mesh?" asks Robert V. Steiner of Teacher's College, Columbia University. "Online courses are more suitable for knowledge-intensive fields like business and engineering," he points out. "Subjects involving skills development and human interaction are more difficult to convey on line." So, for example, in many behavioral sciences courses that involve clinical components, you need to be able to watch human interaction. In many science courses, you need to be able to do lab work. Such courses are more suited to two-way interactive video or on-campus formats than to the online format.

Is the Instructional Technology a Good Match for You?

Your second consideration is whether or not the instructional technology is a good match for your skills, personality, and learning style. In Chapter 2, we covered the pros and cons of the various technologies and described the skills and temperaments best suited to each.

If you are uncertain about your ability to adapt to a program's instructional technology, there are several things you can do. "If possible, take a tour of the technology being used before you enroll," advises Patti Wolf of University of Maryland University College. Many institutional Web sites offer short demos, previews, or tutorials so you can get an idea of what the instructional technology will be like. For example, if you are interested in a distance program at Penn State, you can take a sample course on its World Campus Web site. If the programs in which you are interested do not offer such amenities, ask previous students how the instructional technology worked and what level of expertise is necessary. If technology is an area of particular concern for you, you might even consider a trial run. "I would recommend taking one course before deciding to apply to a school, to see if the style works for the individual," suggests Nicole DeRaleau, an environmental engineering master's degree candidate at Worcester Polytechnic Institute. "If it doesn't work, then perhaps the credits can be transferred and there is no major loss."

"If possible, take a tour of the technology being used before you enroll."

How Reliable Is the Technology?

On a related note, because distance students depend on technology, it's important that it be reliable. Not only will you depend on your own computer, VCR, or television, but you will depend on the institution's technology, too. Ask current students what their experiences have been. Does the server often go down? Are there frequent problems with camera equipment or satellite transmissions?

If the program is newly formatted for distance education, be prepared for some technological bugs to be worked out on your watch. If the prospect of participating in a maiden voyage is too anxiety-provoking, look for programs that have been running for at least a year.

Last, find out what technical support is offered to students. The best setup is free technical support accessed via an 800-number 24 hours a day, seven days a week.

At the best programs, free technical support is available on a 24/7 basis.

How Do the Faculty and Students Interact?

You should also investigate how the communication and social issues involved in distance learning are dealt with in the programs in which you are interested. (For a review of these issues, see Chapter 2.) For example, how do students and faculty members communicate? Will you be expected to log on to an online course at specific times or at your convenience? Will you be expected to participate in online discussions a certain number of times during the course? For example, at the University of Phoenix Online, students are expected to log on and participate five days out of seven. At other schools, participation requirements may be program-wide or set by individual instructors.

Another question to ask is: What is done to overcome the distance learner's social isolation? Some programs do little; others rely on group work to forge a community of learning; and still others use a cohort format, in which a group of students enrolls in a program at the same time and proceeds through it together at the same pace.

Pay particular attention to the faculty-to-student ratio in online courses. If there are more than 25 to 30 students per instructor, you're not likely to get much individual attention.

ADVISING AND OTHER SERVICES

Academic advising is one of the most important student services for distance learners, especially if you are seeking to transfer credits or earn credits through examinations or from life experience to apply to a degree. Check what advising services are offered to distance learners, and see how easy they are to access. "I tested academic advising services," reports a distance learning undergraduate at University of Maryland University College. "That was important to me because I've been out of college for such a long time and I needed some help in selecting courses to complete requirements." Advising is also of particular interest to students in a consortium. If you are interested in a program that is part of a consortium, find out if the consortium offers advising or mentoring to help you navigate among institutions and to guide your overall progress.

Other support services that are important to distance education students are libraries, bookstores, administrative support, record keeping, and technical support (discussed above). Many institutions and consortia offer online and telephone access to these services for distance students. In particular, access to an online library is extremely important, especially if you don't live near a good college or university library. Find out what type of access is offered, what the library's resources are, how materials are delivered, and if training on how to use an online library is offered.

If the program in which you are interested is part of a consortium, be sure you understand how each of these student services is handled. In some cases you will have access only to your home institution's services; in other cases you will have access to the services of all member institutions.

Another thing to watch out for is the extent to which the institution as a whole has kept up with an innovative degree program. For example, at many universities, distance learning courses and programs originate in a couple of departments eager to pursue new ways of educating. However, the university's centralized academic and administrative services may lag behind, leaving distance students to struggle with a system not designed for their needs.

As you investigate a program and its services, keep in mind that the way you are treated as a prospective student can tell you something about what you will encounter once enrolled. "Look at the responsiveness of the institution," advises Robert V. Steiner of Teacher's College, Columbia University, "and ask yourself, 'How client-centered is that program?'"

"Look at the responsiveness of the institution and ask yourself, 'How client-centered is that program?'"

RESIDENCY REQUIREMENT

Some programs, especially doctoral programs, have a residency requirement for distance learning students. The requirement may be several campus visits during the course of a semester, or a brief on-site meeting at the start of a semester. Some residency periods may last up to a week or two. In addition, you may have to travel to campus to take exams, or you may be able to take them locally with a proctor. Be sure you understand what the on-site requirements of a program are, and whether or not you can fulfill them.

TIME FRAMES

Check to see how much time you have to complete a certificate or degree program, and decide whether or not the time frame meets your needs. Some programs have a generous upper limit on the number of years you may take to complete a degree, which allows you to proceed at your own pace. Other programs may be structured on an accelerated or cohort model, with a timetable and lots of interim deadlines. If that's the case, make sure your own schedule can accommodate this. For example, if a program goes year-round and you are usually at a cabin in the woods without Internet access every summer, the program is not a good match for your lifestyle. In addition, if you are considering an accelerated or cohort degree program, make sure you have the support of your family, who may not get much attention from you during this period.

COST

The cost of a distance education degree or certificate program is often the same for on-campus and distance students. However, there are some things you should look out for:

- If you enroll in a consortium, member institutions may charge tuition at different rates.
- If you enroll in a public university, you will probably be charged out-of-state tuition if you are not a state resident.
- Some institutions charge an extra technology fee to cover the costs associated with distance education.
- If there is a residency period, you should plan on spending money for travel, accommodations, and meals.
- If you enroll in an online program, you need to budget for hardware, software, and Internet access as well as books.
- If you are interested in receiving federal financial aid, you must be enrolled in an institution accredited by one of the regional accrediting agencies or certain of the specialized agencies approved by the U.S. Department of Education (check their Web site at www.ed.gov/offices/OPE/accreditation/natlagencies.html).

YOUR PERSONAL CHECKLIST

This chapter discusses many factors that you can consider when evaluating a distance education program. Here is a checklist to sum up the criteria you should keep in mind:

- ✔ The institution's reputation
- ✔ Institutional (regional) accreditation
- ✔ Specialized accreditation, if applicable
- ✔ The program's quality: curriculum, faculty, and responsiveness to adult learners
- ✔ A good match between instructional technology and content
- ✔ A good match between instructional technology and your skills, personality, and learning style
- ✔ Interaction among students and faculty members

✔ Reliability of technology and good technical support
✔ Academic advising services
✔ Other support services: library, bookstore, administrative support, and record keeping
✔ Residency requirements, if any
✔ Time frame for completing certificate or degree
✔ Cost

Although we have described many factors, in the end there may be only three or four aspects of a program that really concern you. You may be more interested in a program's reputation than in any other factor. Or accreditation may be the most important issue for you. Perhaps you are concerned about finding a good match between your personality and learning style and the instructional design of a program. That is why the self-assessment you did while reading Chapter 2 is so crucial, since you can now focus on what's important to you when you evaluate distance programs.

So remember, keep your own educational, professional, and personal needs in the forefront during the selection process. Choosing a good program not only means choosing a high-quality program; it also means choosing a program that's a good match for you.

Taking Standardized Admissions Tests

Chapter 6

For some people, the prospect of taking one of the standardized admissions tests is enough to make them put aside the idea of earning a degree indefinitely. You may be anxious about taking the Scholastic Aptitude Test (SAT I), Graduate Record Examinations (GRE), or one of the professional exams, but if you have chosen to apply to a program that requires an admissions test, there is no way of avoiding the experience. Many undergraduate programs require the SAT I or American College Testing (ACT) Assessment. Graduate programs often require the GRE or a professional examination, and some require a subject area test and writing assessment as well. Finally, if you are not a native speaker of English, you may need to pass a test of English language proficiency. So unless you've chosen to apply to programs that do not require an examination, you are going to have to take at least one exam—and do well on it.

Note that community colleges and many programs designed specifically for adult learners, including some distance learning programs, do not require a standardized admissions test as part of the application process. Therefore, the first thing you should do is to determine which exam(s), if any, you are expected to take. This information should appear in the packet that accompanies the program's application form. If you do not yet have this material, you should simply call the admissions office or program and ask or check the program's Web site. Once you know which exam you must take, contact the testing service that gives the exam and request registration materials or register on line. Information on contacting the testing services appears in the Appendix.

Before we go into detail about the tests, it might be helpful to discuss how an admissions committee might use your score. The role played by the SAT I or ACT Assessment on the undergraduate level is similar to the GRE or GMAT on the graduate level. These tests provide a benchmark. Essentially, your test score is one of the few objective bits of information in your application that can be used to gauge where you fall in the range of applicants. A few programs, especially the top professional programs that receive many more applicants than they can admit, may use the score as a means of reducing the applicant pool. If your score is below their cutoff, they will not even look at the rest of your application. But most programs are much more flexible in the way they evaluate scores. If your score is low, you may still be considered for admission, especially if your grade point average is high, your work experience is relevant, or your application is otherwise strong. Others will index your exam score and your grade point average to arrive at a more balanced number. Some programs offer a conditional admission when a standardized exam score is low. In order to earn an unconditional admission, you may have to retake the exam to boost your score or achieve a certain GPA in the first courses you take.

Basically, you should regard taking a standardized admissions test as an opportunity to improve your application. And that means you must take the test with plenty of time left to meet application deadlines (see Chapters 6 and 7 for more information on applying). That way, if you take the test early and are disappointed with the results, you will have time to retake it. Note that test registration deadlines precede test dates by about six weeks and that you must also allow a few weeks after the testing date for score reporting.

You must also prepare. Thorough preparation, including taking practice tests, can add points to your score by refreshing your memory and giving you experience with test taking. Preparation is especially important if you have been out of school for a long time. As one student who had been out of school for twenty years put it, "Logarithms?! Geometry rules?!" If this sounds like you, you may need to do a quick recap of high school mathematics to do well on the mathematics portion of the SAT I, ACT Assessment, GRE, or GMAT. And you may

"Taking a standardized exam after being out of school twenty years was tough," reports one distance graduate student.

have forgotten what test taking is like, but if you study and practice it will help you overcome any weaknesses you may have. We'll discuss ways to prepare for the exams later in the chapter after we describe the various tests.

UNDERGRADUATE ADMISSIONS TESTS

Bachelor's degree programs that require a standardized admissions test will usually accept either the SAT I or the ACT Assessment. Some programs will also require SAT II Subject Tests in specific subjects.

The SAT I: A Test of Reasoning

The SAT I, which is administered by the Educational Testing Service (ETS) for the College Board, tests your verbal and math reasoning skills. These are analytical skills developed over time both in school and at work; the test does not assess your knowledge of specific content areas.

The SAT I is a 3-hour paper test divided into seven sections: three verbal sections, three math sections, and one extra math or verbal section. The sections can appear in any order.

Verbal Sections. The verbal portions of the SAT I test your ability to understand and analyze what you read, see relationships between the parts of a sentence, and recognize relationships between pairs of words. In other words, it tests your language skills. The verbal sections last 15 or 30 minutes, and there are three types of questions:

- Analogy questions test your understanding of vocabulary, including similarities and parallel relationships between words.
- Sentence completion questions assess your ability to understand the meaning of words and to recognize correct grammatical patterns.
- Critical reading questions measure your ability to read, understand, and think analytically about a single reading passage or a pair of passages.

Math Sections. The math sections of the SAT I assess your ability to solve arithmetic, algebra, and geometry problems. The test does not include trigonometry or calculus. Each section lasts 15 or 30 minutes and has three main types of questions:

- 35 multiple-choice questions with five choices test your ability to solve math problems.
- 15 multiple-choice questions with four choices test your understanding of equalities, inequalities, and estimation.
- 10 questions require a student-generated answer.

Note that you are permitted to bring, in the College Board's words, "almost any four-function, scientific, or graphing calculator" to use on the math sections. According to the College Board, students who use a calculator do slightly better because they do not make computational errors.

Tips for Taking the SAT I. It pays to familiarize yourself with the test directions and typical question format beforehand so you don't waste precious testing time trying to figure out what to do (see the section below on test preparation). Because the sections appear in a paper booklet, you can do the questions in a section in any order. For that reason, it makes sense to answer the easy questions first and place a check mark beside the hard questions. Later, if you have time, you can return to the hard questions.

The way the SAT I is scored should also influence your approach. First, you are awarded one point for each correct answer. But you lose a fraction of a point for each incorrect answer, except on the student-response questions in the math section. On those questions, you do not lose points for an incorrect answer. If you omit a question, you are not penalized. This means that guessing is only worth it if you can eliminate one or two choices as clearly wrong, improving your odds of picking the correct answer. So if a question and its choices are truly mysterious to you, skip it. The test booklet can be used for computations and notes. Don't make any extra marks on the answer sheet, because it's read by a machine that cannot tell the difference between an answer and a doodle.

If you are completely stumped by a question on the SAT I, skip it. You are not penalized for omitting a question.

The SAT II: Subject Tests

The SAT II exams are 1-hour subject area tests that assess your knowledge of a particular content area taught in high school. The questions are primarily multiple-choice. The subject areas include literature in English, writing, U.S. history, world history, two mathematics tests, biology, chemistry, and physics. There are reading-only language tests in French, German, modern Hebrew, Italian, Latin, and Spanish. Finally, there are reading and listening language tests in Chinese, French, German, Japanese, Korean, Spanish, and English Language Proficiency.

ACT Assessment

The ACT Assessment, commonly known as the ACT, is an admissions exam consisting of four tests: English, reading, mathematics, and science reasoning. The examination takes about 3½ hours, and it includes 215 multiple-choice questions with either four or five answer choices. Since you are not penalized for an incorrect answer on the ACT, you should answer all the questions even if you have to guess.

Unlike the SAT I, the ACT is not an aptitude test. Instead, it is based on the high school English, math, and science curriculum. The questions are directly related to what you learned in high school.

GRADUATE ADMISSIONS TESTS

If you apply to graduate school, you may need to take one of the graduate admissions tests. There are three types of Graduate Record Examinations: the General Test, which is usually referred to as the GRE; the subject tests; and the Writing Assessment. Each of these tests has a different purpose, and you may need to take more than one of them. If so, try not to schedule two tests on the same day. The experience may be more arduous than you anticipate. Another general admissions test that is sometimes required instead of the GRE is the Miller Analogies Test. In addition, there are specialized exams required for admission to various professional programs.

The General Test (GRE)

According to ETS, the GRE "measures verbal, quantitative, and analytical reasoning skills that have been developed over a long period of time and are not necessarily related to any field of study." Like the SAT, the GRE is a test designed to assess whether or not you have the aptitude for higher-level study. Even though the GRE may not have subject area relevance, it can indicate that you are capable of doing the difficult reading, synthesizing, and writing demanded of most graduate students.

The test, which is given only on computer, is divided into three separately timed parts, and all the questions are multiple-choice: (1) a 30-minute verbal section with 30 questions, (2) a 45-minute quantitative section with 28 questions, and (3) a 60-minute analytical section with 35 questions. The parts may be presented in any order. In addition, an unidentified verbal, quantitative, or analytical section that doesn't count in your score may be included. You won't have any way to tell which of the duplicated sections is the "real" one, so you should complete both carefully. Finally, another section, on which ETS is still doing research, may also appear. This section will be identified as such and will not count toward your score. ETS tells test takers to plan to spend about 4½ hours at the testing site.

Verbal Section. The thirty questions in the verbal section of the GRE test your ability to recognize relationships between words and concepts, analyze sentences, and analyze and evaluate written material. In other words, they test your vocabulary and your reading and thinking skills. There are four main types of questions in this section:

- In sentence completion questions, sentences are presented with missing word(s). You are asked to select the words that best complete the sentences. Answering correctly involves figuring out the meanings of the missing words from their context in the sentence.
- Analogy questions present a pair of words or phrases that are related to one another. Your task is to figure out the relationship between the two words or phrases. Then you must select the pair of words or phrases whose relationship is most similar to that of the given pair.
- In antonym questions, you are given a word and asked to select the word that is most opposite in meaning.
- Reading comprehension questions test your ability to understand a reading passage and synthesize information on the basis of what you've read.

The words and reading material on which you are tested in this section come from a wide range of subjects, from daily life to the sciences and humanities.

Quantitative Section. This section of the GRE tests your basic mathematical skills and your understanding of elementary mathematical concepts. You will be tested on your ability to reason quantitatively and solve quantitative problems. There are three main types of questions in this section:

- Quantitative comparison questions require that you determine which of two quantities is the larger, if possible. If such a determination is not possible, then you must so indicate.
- Data analysis questions provide you with a graph or a table on which to base your solution to a problem.
- Problem-solving questions test a variety of mathematical concepts. They may be word problems or symbolic problems.

The quantitative questions test your knowledge of arithmetic and high school algebra, geometry, and data analysis. They do not cover trigonometry or calculus.

Analytical Section. According to ETS, the analytical section of the GRE "tests your ability to understand structured sets of relationships, deduce new information from sets of relationships, analyze and evaluate arguments, identify central issues and hypotheses, draw sound inferences, and identify plausible causal relationships." In other words, can you reason analytically and logically? There are two main types of questions in this section:

- Analytical reasoning questions appear in groups, and they are all based on the same set of conditions or rules. A situation is described and you are told how many people or things you will be manipulating. Then you are asked to manipulate the items according to the conditions. For example, you may be given information about a group of people and then asked to rank them in order of age.

- Logical reasoning questions consist of arguments that you must analyze and evaluate. Each argument has assumptions, facts, and conclusions, and you must answer questions that test your ability to assess these.

The subject matter in the analytical section is drawn from all fields of study as well as everyday life.

Tips for Taking the GRE. The GRE is now given only in computer format, and the test is somewhat different from the old paper-and-pencil test. At the start of each section, you are given questions of moderate difficulty. The computer uses your responses to each question and its knowledge of the test's structure to decide which question to give you next. If your responses continue to be correct, how does the computer reward you? It gives you a harder question. On the other hand, if you answer incorrectly, the next question will typically be easier. In short, the computer uses a cumulative assessment of your performance along with information about the test's design to decide which question you get next.

One result of this format is that you cannot skip a question. The computer needs your answer to a question before it can give you the next one. So you have no choice. You must answer or you get a "no score." In addition, this format means you cannot go back to a previous question to change your answer. The computer has already taken your answer and used it to give you subsequent questions. No backtracking is possible once you've entered and confirmed your answer. What this also means is that each person's test is different. Even if two people start with the same item set in the basic test section, once they differ on an answer, the subsequent portion of the test will branch differently.

According to ETS, even though people take different tests, their scores are comparable. This is because the characteristics of the questions answered correctly and incorrectly, including their difficulty levels, are taken into account in the calculation of the score. In addition, ETS claims that the computer-based test scores are also comparable to the old paper-and-pencil test scores.

One benefit of the computer-based format is that when you finish you can cancel the test results—before seeing them—if you feel you've

You cannot skip a question on the computer-based GRE. The computer needs your answer to decide what question to give you next.

Game Plan for Distance Learning

done poorly. If you do decide to keep the test, then you can see your unofficial scores right away. In addition, official score reporting is relatively fast—ten to fifteen days.

A drawback of the format, besides the fact that you cannot skip around, is that some of the readings, graphs, and questions are too large to appear on the screen in their entirety. You have to scroll up and down to see the whole item. Likewise, referring back to a passage or graph while answering a question means that you must scroll up. In addition, you can't underline sentences in a passage or make marks in the margin as you could on the paper test. To make up for this, ETS provides scratch paper that you can use to make notes and do calculations.

To help test takers accustom themselves to the computerized format, ETS provides a tutorial that you complete before starting on the actual test. The tutorial familiarizes you with the use of a mouse, the conventions of pointing, clicking, and scrolling and the format of the test. If you are familiar with computers, the tutorial will take you less than half an hour. If you are not, you are permitted to spend more time on it. According to ETS, the system is easy to use, even for a person with no previous computer experience. However, if you are not accustomed to computers, you would be far better off if you practice your basic skills before you get to the testing site. Although in theory a mouse is easy to use, novices often have trouble getting the cursor to go where they want it to go. The last thing you want to deal with while taking the GRE is a wild mouse and accidental clicking on the wrong answers. If it's any consolation, no knowledge of the keyboard is required—everything is accomplished by pointing and clicking.

GRE Subject Area Tests

The subject area tests are achievement tests, and they test your content knowledge of a particular subject. There are eight subject area tests, and they are given in paper-and-pencil format only. The subjects include biochemistry, cell and molecular biology; biology; chemistry; computer science; literature in English; mathematics; physics; and psychology. The subject area tests assume a level of knowledge consistent with majoring in a subject or at least having an extensive background in it. ETS suggests allowing about 3½ hours at the testing site when taking a subject area test.

Unlike the General Test, which is given many times year round, the subject tests are given only three times a year. Keep in mind that because the tests are paper-based, it takes four to six weeks for your scores to be mailed to your designated institutions. Because the tests are given infrequently and score reporting is slow, be sure you plan ahead carefully so your test results will arrive before your deadlines.

The Writing Assessment

Introduced in 1999 by ETS, the Writing Assessment is a performance-based assessment of critical reasoning skills and analytical writing. It can be taken in computer or paper formats and consists of two parts:

- In the 45-minute "Present Your Perspective on an Issue" task, you must address an issue from any point of view and provide examples and reasons to explain and support your perspective. You are given a choice of two essay topics.
- In the 30-minute "Analyze an Argument" task, you must critique an argument by telling how well reasoned it is. There is no choice of topics in this section.

Scoring of the Writing Assessment is done according to a seven-point scale (0 is the worst; 6 is the best) by college and university faculty members with experience in teaching writing or writing-intensive courses. Each essay is scored independently by two readers. If the two scores are not identical or adjacent, a third reader will be used. The reported score is the average of your two essay scores. If you think the score is unfair, you may request a rescoring.

Miller Analogies Test

The Miller Analogies Test (MAT), which is run by The Psychological Corporation, is accepted by over 2,300 graduate school programs. It is a test of mental ability given entirely in the form of analogies. For example, the analogies may tap your knowledge of fine arts, literature, mathematics, natural science, and social science.

On the MAT, you have 50 minutes to solve 100 problems. The test is given on an as-needed basis at more than 600 test centers in the United States.

Professional School Exams

Professional graduate programs are likely to require you to take the appropriate graduate admissions test. The major tests are the Graduate Management Admissions Test (GMAT), for business school applicants; the Law School Admissions Test (LSAT), for law school applicants; and the Medical College Admissions Test (MCAT), for medical school applicants. However, there are also specialized graduate admissions tests in the fields of dentistry, veterinary science, pharmacy, optometry, and education.

Graduate Management Admissions Test. The test most likely to be taken by prospective distance learning students is the GMAT. It is run by the Graduate Management Admissions Council and administered by ETS. Like the GRE, the GMAT is a computer-based test. It is designed to help schools of business assess applicants' aptitude for graduate level programs in business and management.

The GMAT tests verbal, quantitative, and analytic writing skills:

- In the verbal section, you will be asked to understand and evaluate written English. There are 41 multiple-choice questions of three basic types: reading comprehension, critical reasoning, and sentence correction.
- The quantitative section tests your basic math skills, understanding of elementary mathematical concepts, and ability to solve quantitative problems. There are 37 multiple-choice questions of two basic types: data sufficiency (is there enough information to answer the question?) and problem solving.
- The analytical writing assessment measures your ability to think critically and communicate in writing. There are two essay topics, and you are allowed 30 minutes to respond to each. You must analyze an issue and an argument in this section of the test.

TESTS OF ENGLISH LANGUAGE PROFICIENCY

Regardless of whether you're applying to an undergraduate or graduate program, if your native language is not English, you may be required to take the Test of English as a Foreign Language (TOEFL) or Test of Spoken English (TSE) in order to determine your readiness to take courses in English. Both tests are administered by ETS.

The TOEFL is given in computer-based form throughout most of the world. Like the computer-based GRE, the TOEFL does not require previous computer experience. You are given the opportunity to practice on the computer before the test begins. The TOEFL has four sections—listening, reading, structure, and writing—and it lasts about 4 hours.

The TSE evaluates your ability to speak English. During the test, which takes about a half an hour, you answer questions that are presented in written and recorded form. Your responses are recorded; there is no writing required on this test. The TSE is not given in as many locations as the TOEFL, so you may have to travel a considerable distance to take it.

PREPARING FOR A STANDARDIZED TEST

**Preparing for a
standardized test
will at the very least
familiarize you with
the test instructions
and the types of
questions you will
be asked.**

You can improve your scores and reduce your test anxiety by preparing for the exams you need to take. At the very least, preparation will mean that you are familiar with the test instructions and the types of questions you will be asked. If your computer skills need improvement, adequate preparation will mean that you focus on the questions rather than struggle with the mouse when you take the computer-based tests. For achievement tests such as the subject area tests, you will actually need to study content. There are many ways you can prepare for the tests, but whichever method you choose, start early.

- **Practice by taking old tests.** You can check the Web sites of the various tests to download or request practice tests, or you can buy practice test books at a bookstore. You'll find free sample test questions on many other Web sites, including Peterson's (http://www.petersons.com).

- **Use test preparation workbooks.** These books give information and test taking strategies, as well as practice items. There are many workbooks on the market, some with CD-ROMs, that will help you prepare for an admissions test. You'll find a long list of titles to choose from in Peterson's online bookstore at http://www. petersons.com.

- **Use test preparation software.** Test preparation software is becoming more popular as more of the tests shift to computerized format. You can purchase the software in just about any computer software store. You can also take practice tests online at http:// www.petersons.com/testprep.

- **Take a test preparation course.** If you don't trust yourself to stick with a self-study program using practice tests, workbooks, or software, sign up for a review course such as those given by Kaplan. Although the courses are much more expensive than the do-it-yourself approach, they may be worth it if they make you study.

- **If your math is rusty, study math content.** According to the College Board, people who study math boost their scores more than people who focus only on test taking skills.

For a list of test preparation resources, see the Appendix.

REDUCING TEST ANXIETY

The best way to reduce test anxiety is to be thoroughly prepared. If you are well-acquainted with the format, directions, and types of questions you will encounter, you will not need to waste precious testing time puzzling over these aspects of the exam. In addition to thorough preparation, here are some suggestions to reduce the stress of taking the exam.

- Get a good night's rest and don't tank up on caffeinated beverages— they will only make you feel more stressed.
- Make sure you've got all the things you will need, including your admission ticket and proper identification; pencils and erasers if you are taking a paper based test; and a calculator, if one is permitted.
- Dress in layers so you will be prepared for a range of room temperatures.

- Get to the testing site at least a half an hour early. Make sure you know the way and leave yourself plenty of time to get there.
- Pace yourself during the exam. Know how the exam is scored so you can plan your approach.

Last, try to keep things in perspective. Remember, the exam score is just one item on your application. We'll discuss the remaining parts of an application in the next chapter.

Applying for Admission to Degree Programs

Chapter 7

Now that you have narrowed your selection of programs and ascertained whether or not you need to take a standardized admissions test, it's time to prepare and assemble your applications. If you have not already done so, request an application and information packet from each program to which you plan to apply, download these items from their Web sites, or review them on line.

When you look over these materials, you will see that there may be a lot of work involved in applying to a degree program. It may take you a few months to register for and take standardized tests and to assemble and submit all the necessary information, especially if you're an international student or you've been out of school for a few years. Because the process can be complicated and time consuming, you should start well ahead of time. Even if you apply to a certificate program or an associate's degree program at a community college, a process that is typically less complicated, you should still make sure to start in time.

DEADLINES

For programs at traditional colleges and universities, application deadlines for fall admission may range from August (one full year prior to your planned enrollment) to late spring or summer for programs with rolling admissions. However, most programs require that you submit your application between January and March of the year in which you wish to start. For certificate programs and at community colleges, the deadlines may be later.

At some of the online universities, students can start their studies at any time of year. For example, at Walden University you can start on

> **Making a checklist of your application items and deadlines can help you keep track of them.**

the first of any month. At Walden, the deadline for application materials is the first of the month two months prior to the month of enrollment.

Different programs have different deadlines. So be careful when you check the deadlines in the application materials from your various programs. And remember, the deadlines are not suggestions. One student applying to a traditional university who mistook a March deadline for May recalls that "not only would they not consider my application, but they wouldn't refund my application fee, either. I had to reapply the next year and pay again to be considered for their program." So don't be careless about dates—double-check them. Make a checklist like Figure 7-1 to help you keep track of things and stay on top of deadlines.

Application Checklist. Keep track of your applications by inserting a check mark or a completion date in the appropriate column or row. Note that the last four items are financial aid documents, which will be discussed in Chapter 8.

PARTS OF AN APPLICATION

For each program to which you apply, you will have to submit a number of items to make your application complete. For most bachelor's and graduate degree programs, these include:

- Standardized admissions test scores (see Chapter 6)
- An application form
- Your high school, undergraduate, or other transcripts
- Letters of recommendation
- Personal essay(s)

In addition, if you are seeking credit for life experience, an assessment portfolio will be required (see Chapter 3). A personal interview may be required for some programs, although for most, an interview is optional. A program may require additional items, such as a resume or arts portfolio.

For most associate degree programs at community colleges, the application is much simpler. Typically, it consists of just an application

Figure 7–1: Application Checklist

Item	Program 1	Program 2	Program 3
	Date Due/Date Completed	Date Due/Date Completed	Date Due/Date Completed
Application form			
Test scores requested			
Transcripts requested			
Letters of recommendation solicited			
Letters of recommendation follow up			
Personal essay(s)			
Application fee			
Other items required (specify)			
Application submitted			
Application follow up			
FAFSA			
Other financial aid forms			
Financial aid supporting documents			
Financial aid application follow up			

form; you may not even need to submit high school transcripts. For certificate programs, the application may consist of an application form and one or two other items.

Because requirements vary so widely, be sure you read the admissions information thoroughly so you understand what each program expects of you. Since each program may require a slightly different set of items, be sure your checklist reflects this in order to keep track of what you'll need to do.

We'll discuss the main elements of an application below; we'll cover financial aid applications in the next chapter.

THE APPLICATION FORM

On the application form, you provide basic information such as the program or department to which you are applying; your name, date of birth, social security number, address, and contact information; your citizenship status; your demographic background (usually optional); your current employer and position; your educational background; names of people who are providing references (ask them first!); and admissions test dates. Sometimes the application form also includes a section for applying for financial aid. However, a separate application form for financial aid may be necessary. Be sure you understand what forms you need to submit and to whom if you are applying for aid.

If you use a paper application, you should type the information on the form. If a typewriter is not available, then print your entries neatly. Be sure you do not accidentally omit information, and double-check that there are no spelling errors. "Photocopy the application and fill the copy out," suggests Nicole DeRaleau, a graduate student in engineering at Worcester Polytechnic Institute. "Make sure it is clear and concise, and then copy it onto the actual form."

If you decide to apply on line, don't just sit at the computer and dash off the application. Download the application form, fill it in, then proofread it carefully. Only then should you transmit it, being sure to keep a copy. Note that if you apply to an online degree program and the school does not offer an online application, you should think twice about applying. The lack of an online application is probably indicative of the low level of online student services you can expect once you are enrolled.

Many undergraduate colleges accept a common application form in place of their own. This means that most of the fields you will need to fill in will be the same for all of the schools that accept the common application. You may have to fill out a supplementary form for a college if you use one of these standardized forms. Using a standardized application form lets you concentrate on being organized and writing good essays.

TRANSCRIPTS

As proof of your academic background, you will need to submit official transcripts from each high school (for undergraduate programs), college, and university you have attended, even if you have taken just one course from that institution. To request official transcripts, contact your high school's guidance office or the registrars of your undergraduate college and other institutions you have attended. Be sure to allow two or three months for your request to be processed. It will save time if you call ahead to find out what the fee for each transcript is and what information they need to pull your file and send the transcript to the proper recipient. Then you can enclose a check for that amount with your written request.

Since many schools will send the transcripts directly to the admissions offices of the programs to which you are applying, you may also want to request an unofficial copy of your transcript. You can use this copy for your own reference during the application process.

When you review your transcripts, look for weaknesses that may need explaining, even if they occurred years ago. For example, a low GPA one semester, a very poor grade in a course, or even a below-average overall GPA may hurt your chances of acceptance unless you have a good reason for them. You can explain any shortfalls in your transcripts in your personal essay, cover letter, or addendum to the application.

LETTERS OF RECOMMENDATION

You will probably have to provide letters of recommendation for each program to which you apply. These letters are important, because like the personal essay, they give the members of the admissions committee

If you use one of the online common application forms, you may have to submit a supplementary form as well.

a more personal view of you than is possible from your grades and test scores. Good letters of recommendation can tremendously increase your chances of admission, and lukewarm letters can harm your application. So it's important to approach the task of choosing and preparing your letter writers in a thoughtful and timely fashion.

In fact, it's a good idea to start asking for references a few months before your application deadline. Professionals and professors are extremely busy people, and the more time that you can give them to work on your recommendation, the better it will reflect who you are. Starting early will also give you an opportunity to follow up with your recommenders well before the application deadlines.

Ask people for letters of recommendation well before they are due to give them plenty of time to prepare them.

Choosing People to Write Recommendations

If possible, at least one of your recommendations should be from a teacher or professor, because (1) they are in the best position to judge you as a potential student and (2) members of the admissions committee will consider them peers and so be more inclined to trust their judgment of you.

If you cannot make up the full complement of letters from faculty members or if you are applying to professional programs, you can ask employers or people who know you in a professional capacity to write references for you. In fact, if you are applying to professional programs, having letters of recommendation from those already practicing in the field is a plus.

When you are trying to decide whom to ask for recommendations, keep these criteria in mind. The people you ask should

- have a high opinion of you.
- know you well, preferably in more than one context.
- be familiar with your field.
- be familiar with the programs to which you apply.
- have taught a large number of students (or have managed a large number of employees) so they have a good basis upon which to compare you (favorably!) to your peers.
- be known by the admissions committee as someone whose opinion can be trusted.
- have good writing skills.

- be reliable enough to write and mail the letter on time.

A tall order? Yes. It's likely that no one person you choose will meet all these criteria, but try to find people who come close to this ideal.

Approaching Your Letter Writers

Once you've decided whom you plan to ask for references, be diplomatic. Don't simply show up in their offices, ask them to write a letter, and give them the letter of recommendation forms. Plan your approach so that you leave the potential recommender, as well as yourself, a graceful "out" in case the recommender reacts less than enthusiastically.

On your first approach, you should remind the person about who you are (if necessary) and then ask if they think they can write you a good letter of recommendation. This gives the person a chance to say no. If the person agrees, but hesitates or seems to be lukewarm, you can thank them for agreeing to help you. Later, you can write them a note saying that you won't need a letter of recommendation after all. On the other hand, if the person seems genuinely pleased to help you, you can then make an appointment to give them the letter of recommendation forms and the other information they will need.

Waiving Your Right to See a Letter

The letter of recommendation forms in your application packets contain a waiver. If you sign the waiver, you give up your right to see the letter of recommendation. Before you decide whether or not to sign it, discuss the waiver with each person who is writing you a reference. Some people will write you a reference only if you agree to sign the waiver and they can be sure the letter is confidential. This does not necessarily mean they intend to write a negative letter; instead, it means that they think a confidential letter will carry more weight with the admissions committee. In fact, they are right. A confidential letter usually has more validity in the eyes of the admissions committee. From the committee's point of view, an "open" letter may be less than candid because the letter writer knew you were going to read it. So, in general, it's better for you to waive your right to see a letter. If this makes you anxious in regard to a particular recommender, then do not choose that person to write a letter.

Helping Your Letter Writers

Once a faculty member or employer has agreed to write a letter of recommendation for you, he or she wants to write something positive on your behalf. No matter how great you are, this won't be possible if the letter writer cannot remember you and your accomplishments very well.

So when you meet with your letter writers to give them the letter of recommendation forms, use this opportunity to provide them with information about yourself. Bring a resume that highlights your academic, professional, and personal accomplishments. List the course or courses you took with them, the grades you got, and any significant work you did, such as a big research paper or presentation. The resume can be the basis of a conversation you have with the letter writer that amplifies your notable accomplishments.

What should you do if the letter writer asks *you* to draft the letter? Accept gracefully. Then pretend you are the writer, and craft a letter extolling your virtues and accomplishments in detail. Remember, if the letter writer does not like what you've written, he or she is free to change it in the final draft.

You can help your letter writers by filling in as much of the information as you can on the letter of recommendation forms. It's also a nice gesture to provide stamped, addressed envelopes for the letters if they are to be mailed directly to the programs or to you for inclusion in your application. Be sure your letter writers understand what their deadlines are. In other words, do everything you can to expedite the process, especially since you may be approaching people who are already extremely busy.

Last, send thank-you notes to professors and employers who have come through for you with letters of recommendation. Cementing good relationships now can only help you in the future.

If You've Been Out of School for Years

What should you do if you have been out of school for years and have lost touch with your teachers and professors? There are several things you can do to overcome the problems associated with the passage of time.

First, if a teacher or professor is still at your alma mater, you can get in touch by mail or e-mail, remind the person of who you are, describe what you've done since they taught you and what your plans for school are, and include a resume. Tell the instructor what you remember most about the courses you took with him or her. Most people keep their course records for at least a few years and can look up your grades. If you are still near your high school or undergraduate institution, you can make your approach in person. Once you've made this initial approach, you can then call and ask if the person thinks he or she can write a strong recommendation for you.

Another strategy if you've been out of school for a while is to obtain letters of recommendation from faculty members teaching in the programs to which you plan to apply. In order to obtain such a letter, you may have to take a course in the program before you enroll so that the faculty member gets to know you. Members of an admissions committee will hesitate to reject a candidate who has been strongly recommended by one of their colleagues.

Finally, if you are having trouble recruiting teachers and professors to recommend you, call the programs to which you are applying and ask what their policy is for applicants in your situation. Many programs designed for adult learners, especially the professional programs, allow you to use letters from employers. But remember, if you apply to an academic rather than a professional program, letters from employers will not carry as much weight as letters from faculty members.

THE PERSONAL ESSAY

The application to a degree program is not all numbers and outside evaluations. Schools are also interested in finding out about you as an individual and in more intangible qualities, like your ability to write a good essay. Thus, the personal essay is the part of the application in which you can take control and demonstrate who you are and why you deserve to be admitted. Other parts of your application—test scores, grade point average, and transcripts—may reflect your academic ability, but not much else. The letters of recommendation are beyond your control once you've chosen the writers. But a good personal essay can make you stand out. It can show the qualities that will make you an excellent student and professional. In other words, the essay is your showcase and you should make the most of it. Even if you can write superb prose in your sleep, you still need to know *what* to write. In this section, you'll get a step-by-step guide to preparing the personal essay.

The personal essay is your showcase, so you should make the most of it.

Requirements Vary

The essays required of applicants vary widely. For some programs, you may just have to explain in one or two paragraphs why you want to go to that school. For others, you may have to write on a more creative topic, such as the person who influenced you the most. Still for others, such as graduate business programs, the application may call for two, three, or even more essays on different topics. Business schools and programs pay a lot of attention to the personal essay because professional experience is an important criterion for admission, and this is best reflected in the essays.

The admissions committee gleans a lot of information from *what* you write. But they can also tell a lot from *how* you write. If your writing is clear and conveys your ideas effectively, you are demonstrating your ability to communicate. If your writing is free of grammatical and spelling errors, you are demonstrating your attention to detail. Good writing skills are essential for a student in any field, so a poorly written essay can hurt an application. A well-written statement, on the other hand, will help your case.

Think Before You Write

Do you remember the self-assessment you did in Chapter 2? You answered many difficult questions about your goals, interests, strengths, and weaknesses in order to decide if pursuing an education through distance learning was right for you. If you did an honest and thorough job of assessing yourself then, you will have already thought through many of the issues you will now need to address when you write your personal essay.

Things to Think About. Your self-assessment should make it easier for you to get a handle on issues such as:

- your personal and professional goals and their relationship to your education
- how you came to be interested in a particular field and why you think you are well suited for it
- aspects of your life that make you uniquely qualified to pursue study in this field
- experiences or qualities that distinguish you from other applicants
- unusual hardships or obstacles that you've had to overcome
- unusual accomplishments, whether personal, professional, or academic
- professional experiences that have contributed to your personal growth
- how your skills and personal characteristics would contribute to your success in a distance learning degree program

In addition, when you researched and evaluated programs to which you would apply, you learned a lot about the programs that were good matches for you. In your essay, you may also have to address issues like

- what appeals to you about a particular program.
- how your interests and strengths match their needs.

Be Yourself . . . The most common piece of advice from most admissions directors about writing the personal essay is to be yourself. Remember, you are seeking to be accepted by a program that is a good match for you. If you disguise who you really are in an effort to impress an admissions committee, you are doing yourself—and the school—a disservice. So, be honest. If you demonstrate self-knowledge by presenting your strengths as well as your limitations, your essay will be a true reflection of who you are.

. . . But Be Diplomatic. Honesty is important, but so is diplomacy. Try not to reveal weaknesses in your personality such as laziness, dishonesty, or selfishness. Don't say you want to enroll in a program just because it's on line or you know you can get in. Even though these things may be true, they are not reasons with which the admissions committee will necessarily be sympathetic. Instead, frame your points in a positive light: you can fulfill the admission requirements because you have the proper prerequisites, and you know of its reputation for quality online teaching.

Write a Strong Opening

When you write your essay, put yourself in the position of an admissions committee member who may be reading fifty essays a day. By the end of all this reading, this poor individual may be bored to tears and would be pleased by any essay that simply engages his or her interest. How are you going to accomplish this? By writing an opening that grabs the reader's attention.

Describe an Important Experience. Instead of beginning with, "I want to go to school because . . ." try to engage the reader with something significant. For example, was there an experience that led you to make the decision to pursue your education? If so, describe it.

The opening is also the place where you can set forth any unusual experience you have had that contributed significantly to the person you are today. The experience may be growing up poor, being an Olympic athlete, or moving to the United States at the age of fourteen. Whatever the experience is, show how it has formed your character and life and how it relates to the education you want to pursue now.

Be Specific. What if you have not had a defining moment or experience that sparked your interest in further education? Then write an opening that is specific enough to have some real interest. The key is to remember that specific details are usually more interesting than general statements. Use concrete examples of your successes and action verbs to describe events. Be specific and you'll have a better chance of connecting with your readers.

Tell How Your Story Intersects With Theirs

If you apply to several programs, you will be tempted to write a boilerplate essay. Resist the temptation. Admissions committees grow adept at picking out the generic personal statements.

Remember that when you were evaluating programs you were looking for a good match for you. The personal essay is the place where you can explain to the admissions committee why you are a good match for that school. The story of your intellectual and professional development and your goals should culminate in your reasons for choosing this particular program. Your reasons should reflect a knowledge of the program.

Use the Brochure or Catalog as a Resource. You can use the knowledge you've gained from researching the program if you don't know it firsthand to explain why you want to enroll in a program. In particular, the program brochure or catalog can be a good resource when you write this section of the essay. It's important to know what a school has to offer before you write the essay. The admissions committee members will be looking for a good fit for their program.

In addition to identifying the tangible characteristics of a program, you can also get a sense of its philosophy and values from the brochure or catalog.

The personal essay is the place where you can explain to the admissions committee why you are a good match for that school.

Describe Your Goals

In most essays, you will have to explain how a degree will help you achieve your goals. Even if you are not exactly sure what you want to do professionally, describe what you might be interested in doing once you receive the degree. Indicating that you have a purpose in obtaining a degree shows that you are focused and motivated and have a real sense of the possibilities.

Explain Shortcomings in Your Background

There is a difference of opinion on whether or not the personal essay is the place to explain any weaknesses in your academic or professional preparation if you are not directly asked to do so. Some people think that the essay should concentrate on a positive presentation of your qualifications. They feel that an explanation of poor standardized test scores, for example, belongs in an addendum or cover letter. Others think that the essay is the place to address your application's weaknesses.

Perhaps a good rule of thumb is to address any weaknesses or shortcomings that are directly relevant to your proposed studies in the essay. On the other hand, if the weak spot in your application is not directly related to your field of study, you may prefer to address it in an addendum or cover letter. For example, if when you were a college freshman you had a poor GPA, you can explain this separately. Try to put a positive spin on it, too. Explain, for example, how your GPA in your major was much higher, or how your GPA improved as you matured. Essentially, your decision as to where to address your weaknesses will depend on their importance and relevance to your pursuit of a degree.

Edit Your Drafts

Follow the Instructions. When you sit down to draft your essay, the first thing you should make sure is that you are *answering the question posed on the application*. Be sure you read the instructions for each program's personal statement carefully. Small differences in wording can affect how you approach writing the essay.

When you sit down to draft your essay, the first thing you should make sure is that you are *answering the question posed on the application*.

Don't Write Too Much or Too Little. The second thing you should keep in mind as you begin your draft is the length of the essay. Often, the length is specified. What should you do if length is not specified? Write one to two typed pages. An essay that is shorter than one page does not allow room for you to develop your ideas, and an essay that is longer than two pages becomes a chore for the admissions committee to read. Don't play with font size, either, in order to get the statement to come out the right length. Admissions officers don't really want to read eight-point type. Stick with a basic font, such as Times New Roman, and keep the size between 10 and 12 points. If the essay asks for a specific word count, follow it to the letter. If you come in over or under by 10 words or so, don't worry too much about it. But if you're 100 or more words short or long, you'll have some adding or cutting to do.

Finally, when you write your first draft, do not waste space by repeating information that the admissions committee can get from other parts of your application like your transcript or resume. Use the essay to provide new information or to highlight particular accomplishments.

Review the First Draft. Once you have drafted your essay, read the question again. Has your draft answered the question fully? If the essay is incomplete, go back and fill in the missing material. Then ask people for feedback. Although your spouse and friends may be helpful, you may get more valuable suggestions from faculty members or colleagues who know you and who also know what a personal essay should be like. Ask whether you've included things you should leave out or should add things you've forgotten. Is the tone right? Have you achieved the right balance between boasting and being too modest? Are there any problems with organization, clarity, grammar, or spelling?

Prepare the Final Draft. Once you've revised the essay, set it aside for a couple of days. Then proofread it with a fresh eye. If you are satisfied with your final draft, ask someone else to proofread it for you. The final draft should be absolutely free of grammar and spelling errors, so do not rely on grammar or spellcheckers to find all the errors. Once you are done, be sure to keep backup files as well as a hard copy. Although you won't be able to use the whole essay for all your applications, you may be able to use parts of it. If you do work this way, be absolutely sure when you submit the final essays to different programs that you have not made any embarrassing cutting and pasting mistakes.

Finally, if you submit the statement on separate sheets of paper rather than on the application form itself, put your name, social security number, and the question at the top of the essay and type "see attached essay" on the application form.

Make It Yours

If after reading this section you are still daunted by the prospect of writing your personal statement, just put the whole task aside for a few days. You will find that the ideas and suggestions you've just read will trigger some mental activity and that soon you will have some ideas of your own to jot down.

Remember, also, that it's not necessary to have an exotic background or a dramatic event to recount in order to write a good essay and gain admission to a program. Admissions committees look for diversity—in gender, race, ethnicity, nationality, and socioeconomic status—to name some obvious characteristics. But they are also look for people with diverse life experiences to add richness to their student body. Your background, which may seem perfectly ordinary to you, nevertheless has unique and relevant elements that can be assets to the program you choose. Your task is to identify and build upon these elements to persuade the admissions committee that you should be selected.

INTERVIEWS

Interviews are rarely a requirement of the distance education application process. However, if you think you do well in interviews, you can call each program and ask for an interview. A good interview may be an opportunity to sway the admissions committee in your favor. Human nature being what it is, an excellent half-hour interview may loom larger than years of average grades in the minds of those who evaluate your application.

Most interviewers are interested in the way you approach problems, think, and articulate your ideas, and so they will concentrate on questions that will reveal these aspects of your character and not on questions that test your technical knowledge. They may ask you controversial questions or give you hypothetical problems to solve. Or they may ask about your professional goals, motivation for study, and areas of interest—much the same material that is in a typical personal essay. Remember that interviewers are interested more in how you think than in what you think.

When you prepare for an interview, it would be helpful if you have already written your personal essay, because the thought processes involved in preparing the essay will help you articulate many of the issues that are likely to come up in an interview. It is also helpful to do your homework on the program, so if the opportunity arises for you to ask questions, you can do so intelligently. Last, be sure you are dressed properly. That means dress as if you are going to a professional job interview.

SUBMITTING YOUR APPLICATION

As we mentioned at the beginning of the chapter, you should submit your completed applications well before they are due. *Be sure to keep a copy of everything.* That way, you won't lose hours of work if the application gets lost. You can either mail the application to the admissions office or file portions of it on line through the programs' Web sites. Remember, however, that some elements of the application, such as the fee and official transcripts, will still need to be mailed in paper form. Note also that most schools that accept online applications simply print them and process them as if they had come in by regular mail.

> **Be sure to keep a copy of everything in your application. That way, you won't lose hours of work if it gets lost.**

Try to submit all of your materials at once, which simplifies the task of compiling and tracking your application at the admissions office. If that's impossible, as it is for many students, keep track of missing items and forward them as soon as possible. Remember that if items are missing, your application is likely just to sit in the admissions office.

Following Up

It's important that you check up on the status of your applications, especially if you don't receive acknowledgment that an application is complete. Give the admissions office a couple of weeks to process your application, and then call or send an e-mail to find out whether or not it's complete. For some schools, you can check the status of your application on line through their Web sites. Usually the missing items are transcripts or letters of recommendation.

IN SUMMARY

Preparing a thorough, focused, and well-written application is one of the most important tasks you will ever undertake. A good application can gain you admission to a program that can help you achieve your goals. "The application process is just one of those hoops you have to jump through to get where you want to go," advises a distance learning student at Gonzaga University. With your destination in mind, work on your applications as if they are the most important things you can possibly be doing, because they are.

Paying for Your Education

Chapter 8

Pursuing a certificate or degree can cost a lot of money, but it is usually money well spent. On average, people with undergraduate and graduate degrees make more money than those who do not have these credentials. Still, the question remains: How are you going to pay for school and support yourself (and perhaps your family) at the same time?

Most adult distance learning students solve the problem of paying for their education by continuing to work full-time and attending school part time. As one student put it, "I work and I pay as I go." Although attending part-time does not cut the total cost of your certificate or degree, it does have the advantage of spreading your costs over a longer period and enables you to pay for your education out of your current income. Note, however, that attending school less than half-time will disqualify you from most forms of financial aid.

In this chapter, we'll discuss ways to pay for your education, both by looking for low-cost alternatives and by finding financial aid. We'll discuss types and sources of aid, where you can find information about financial aid, and the application process. Finally, we'll describe some of the tax issues that may be relevant to students pursuing higher education.

LOOKING FOR LOW-COST ALTERNATIVES

There are ways you can cut the cost of your education, even before you look for sources of financial aid. These include attending a community college rather than a four-year college and attending a public institution of higher education rather than a private one.

Community College versus Four-Year College

If you are an undergraduate pursuing a bachelor's degree, you could consider enrolling at a community college for your first two years of study. Most community colleges charge less tuition than four-year

Game Plan for Distance Learning

colleges do. Toward the end of your second year of study, you can apply to a four-year college as a transfer student and complete your bachelor's degree there.

Public versus Private College or University

Since four-year public colleges and universities get most of their support from government funding, they are less expensive than private colleges and universities. Public colleges and universities usually have two scales for tuition and fees—one for out-of-state residents and a much less expensive scale for state residents.

With so much money at stake, and if moving is an option for you, it is definitely worthwhile to find out how you can establish residency in the state in which you plan to get your degree. You may simply have to reside in the state for a year—your first year of school—in order to be considered a legal resident. But being a resident while a student may not count, and you may have to move to the state a year before you plan to enroll. The legal residency requirements of each state vary, so be sure you have the right information if you decide to pursue this strategy.

TYPES OF FINANCIAL AID

Before we get into a discussion of the various sources of financial aid, it would be helpful to understand some basics. For example, financial aid can be classified in a few ways. First, it can be categorized by type of aid:

Grants, scholarships, and fellowships are gifts; loans must be repaid; and work-study awards must be earned.

- **Grants, scholarships,** and **fellowships** are gifts that do not have to be repaid. These words are used somewhat interchangeably; there is no real difference among them, except that scholarships are usually awarded to undergraduates and fellowships are awarded to graduate students.
- **Loans** are awards that do have to be repaid, with interest, either while you are in school or after you leave school, it depends on the terms of the loan. If you consider loans, note that financial aid counselors recommend that your total student debt payment should not exceed 8 to 15 percent of your projected monthly income after you receive your degree.

- **Work-study awards** are amounts you earn through part-time work in a federal aid program.
- **Reimbursements**, generally from employers, repay you for amounts you've already spent on tuition.

You can also classify financial aid according to the reason the student is awarded the aid:

- **Need-based aid** is financial aid awarded on the basis of your financial need. It may take the form of grants, loans, or work-study.
- **Merit-based aid** is funding awarded on the basis of academic merit, regardless of financial need. A subset of merit-based aid is student profile-based aid—financial aid to students because of their identities. For example, some scholarships are targeted for veterans, minorities, or women; and others are targeted for people with very specific qualifications that the philanthropist wants to reward, such as an Eagle Scout studying labor relations.

A third way to classify financial aid is by its source. The major sources of aid for students are as follows:

- The **federal government**, by far the largest disburser of financial aid—over $50 billion to more than 8.5 million students each year
- **State governments**, some of which have large financial aid programs
- **Private sources of aid**, which include colleges and universities, employers, foundations, service organizations, national scholarship and fellowship programs, home equity loans, and private loan programs

The federal government disburses about $50 billion in aid to more than 8.5 million students annually.

THE LANGUAGE OF FINANCIAL AID

There's some financial aid jargon that you'll have to master in order to understand need-based financial aid programs. Some terms that you'll see frequently include the following:

- **Enrollment status**—Whether you are enrolled full-time, three-quarter time, half-time, or less than half-time in a degree or certificate program. Your status affects your eligibility for most types of aid.

- **Expected Family Contribution (EFC)**—The amount you and your family are expected to contribute to the cost of your education per academic year. If you are a dependent, *family* means you and your parents; if you are independent, this means you and your spouse, if you are married. The formula was established by the U.S. Congress to help estimate federal aid amounts for eligible students, and it is used by college financial aid offices as well as the U.S. Department of Education.

- **Cost of attendance**—The total cost—tuition, fees, living expenses, books, supplies, and miscellaneous expenses—of attending a particular school for an academic year. Each school estimates its own cost of attendance, and you can find out what it is if you check your admissions information packet or call the financial aid office. Distance learners should make sure that technology costs are included in the school's cost of attendance and in their own budgets. The cost of transportation, hotels, and meals during residency periods, if any, should also be accounted for in the cost of attendance.

The basic financial aid equation: Cost of Attendance—Expected Family Contribution = Financial Need.

- **Financial need**—The amount of money you need to be given or loaned or that you will earn through work-study in order to attend your school. It is calculated by subtracting your Estimated Family Contribution from your cost of attendance:

  Cost of Attendance
  – Expected Family Contribution
  = Financial Need

Note that your financial need will differ from program to program. That's because the cost of attendance will vary from school to school, but your Expected Family Contribution will remain the same, whether you attend the local community college or an expensive private university.

FEDERAL FINANCIAL AID

As we've mentioned, the U.S. government is the largest player in the financial aid arena, and most of your financial aid is likely to come from this source. The federal government provides need-based aid in the form of grants, work-study programs, and loans. Up-to-date information about federal financial aid programs can be found at the U.S. Department of Education's Web site, www.ed.gov/studentaid, or by calling 800-4-FEDAID (toll-free). Eligibility issues relevant to distance learners and some of the basics of federal aid are discussed below. Note that some of these eligibility criteria may change in the future as distance degrees become more common and financial aid programs are modified to reflect the new realities.

Are You Eligible for Federal Financial Aid?

Your financial need is just one criterion used to determine whether or not you are eligible to receive aid from the federal government. In addition, you must

- have a high school diploma or GED or pass a test approved by the Department of Education.
- be enrolled in a degree or certificate program.
- be enrolled in an eligible institution (see below).
- be a U.S. citizen or eligible noncitizen.
- have a Social Security number.
- register with the Selective Service if required.
- maintain satisfactory academic progress once you are in school.

If you have been convicted under federal or state laws of the sale or possession of illegal drugs, you may not be eligible to participate in federal financial aid programs. Call the Federal Student Aid Information Center at 800-4-FEDAID (toll-free) for further information.

If you are not sure if you qualify as an eligible noncitizen, call the financial aid office of the school you plan to attend.

Institutional Eligibility: An Issue Pertinent to Distance Learners

In order to participate in federal financial aid programs, an institution of higher learning must fulfill the criteria established by Congress for the disbursement of Title IV funds, as federal student aid is officially known. There are many complex regulations that establish institutional eligibility. Of these, several may apply to institutions that offer certificates or degrees at a distance. For example, in order to be eligible to participate in federal financial aid programs, an institution must be accredited by an agency—other than the Distance Education and Training Council (DETC)—recognized by the U.S. Department of Education. The reason that schools accredited only by the DETC are not eligible is that they are classified as "correspondence schools," and schools that teach primarily by correspondence are ineligible according to the law. In order to qualify to disburse Title IV aid, an institution must teach at least 50.1 percent of its classes in the traditional classroom or must be classified as an independent study institution rather than a correspondence school. Other requirements for participation in federal financial aid programs involve the academic schedule; for example, there must be a thirty-week academic year, a template that doesn't fit some of the new virtual universities.

An institution's accreditation status affects its eligibility to participate in federal financial aid programs.

The Distance Education Demonstration Program. The rules governing federal aid were originally promulgated to prevent fraud and to assure that funds would be provided to students at schools that met certain standards. However, with the growth of distance education, these regulations are increasingly becoming obstacles to provide aid to students at legitimate but innovative institutions. Recognizing this, Congress established the Distance Education Demonstration Program under the direction of the Department of Education. "The purpose of the Distance Education Demonstration Program is to collect data that will provide some understanding of what constitutes quality in distance education," explains Marianne R. Phelps, former special assistant to the assistant secretary for postsecondary education. "Congress needs information in order to become comfortable with the risks involved in funding distance education." Under this program, the department is permitted to waive some of the Title IV regulations, if necessary, for the fifteen participating institutions of higher education. Eventually, the experiences and data generated by the Distance Education Demonstration Program may provide a basis for a review of current rules and regulations.

Determining the Eligibility Status of an Institution or Program. In the meantime, what can you do to make sure that the school and program in which you are interested are eligible to participate in federal financial aid programs? The simple answer, of course, is call them and ask. However, you can also do some double-checking on your own to confirm what the school tells you.

If you plan to enroll in a regionally accredited traditional college or university, you can safely assume that the institution as a whole is eligible to participate in federal aid programs—since distance certificates and degrees are likely to be a very small proportion of its overall offerings (see Chapter 5 for a discussion of accreditation). However, because institutions have the discretion to exclude specific programs, you should double-check to see if the school disperses federal aid to students enrolled in programs that interest you. Call the financial aid office and ask. If you are not sure of the accreditation status, and therefore the Title IV status, of the school in which you are interested, first check with the school to find out which agencies, if any, have accredited it. Then visit the Department of Education's Web site to check on the accrediting agencies. The department lists the accrediting agencies of which it approves, and in its short description of each agency, it indicates whether or not the institutions it accredits qualify for Title IV funding. You can then call the accrediting agency to make sure it has indeed accredited the school or program in which you are interested.

> You can safely assume that a regionally accredited institution is eligible to participate in federal aid programs.

Federal Aid Programs

Once you've established the eligibility of the institution and program in which you are interested, you may want to check the federal aid programs in which they participate. Not all schools participate in all the available programs.

Among the federal aid programs are Pell Grants, Federal Supplemental Educational Opportunity Grants, work-study, Federal Family Education Loans (FFEL) and William D. Ford Direct Loans (commonly called Stafford loans), and Perkins Loans.

Pell Grants. Pell Grants, which do not have to be repaid, are awarded to undergraduate students on the basis of need, even if they are enrolled less than half time. In some cases, a student enrolled in a postbaccalaureate teacher certification program may be awarded a Pell Grant. There are no Pell Grants for other graduate students.

The maximum amount of the Pell Grant changes each year and depends on annual funding allocations by Congress. The maximum award for the school year 2000–01 was $3,300. The amount of an award depends on a combination of your financial need, your costs to attend school, your enrollment status as a full-time or part-time student, and whether or not you plan to study for a full academic year or less.

If you are awarded a Pell Grant, the money can be applied directly to your school costs or be paid to you directly or some combination of these methods. Your school must inform you on how it will be disbursing your grant. Disbursements must occur at least once per term or a minimum of twice a year.

Federal Supplemental Educational Opportunity Grants. Federal Supplemental Educational Opportunity Grants (FSEOGs) are awards to undergraduates with exceptional financial need, even if they are enrolled less than half time. These grants generally go to Pell Grant recipients with the lowest Estimated Family Contributions. The amount of an FSEOG ranges from $100 to $4,000 per year.

Unlike the Pell Grant program, which provides funds to each eligible student, the FSEOG program is campus-based. This means that the federal government awards each participating institution a certain amount of money, and the school's financial aid office decides how to allocate it. When the school uses up its funding for the year, there are no more FSEOGs awarded. Check with your school to see whether or not it participates in this program.

Federal Work-Study Program. Some colleges and universities participate in the federal work-study program, which provides part-time jobs in public and private nonprofit organizations to both undergraduate and graduate students who demonstrate financial need. The government pays up to 75 percent of your wages, and your employer pays the balance. The value of a work-study job depends on your need, the other elements in your financial aid package, and the amount of money the school has to offer. Not all universities have work-study funds, and some that do have the funds limit their use to undergraduates.

If you receive work-study funds, you may be able to use them in a job that is related to your field. You will have to check with the financial aid office to find out what jobs are available, whether or not you can use the funds in a job you find elsewhere, and what bureaucratic requirements you will have to satisfy.

Stafford Loan Programs (FFEL and Direct Loans). The Federal Family Education Loan (FFEL) program and the William D. Ford Direct Loan Program, commonly called Stafford loans, are two loan programs sponsored by the federal government. Schools generally participate in one of the two programs. The terms and conditions of these loans are similar; the major differences are the source of the funds and some repayment provisions. If you get a FFEL, your funds will come from a bank, credit union, or other participating lender. If you get a Direct Loan, the money comes directly from the federal government.

You are eligible to borrow under these loan programs if you are enrolled at least half time and have financial need remaining after your Estimated Family Contribution, Pell Grant eligibility, and aid from other sources are subtracted from your annual cost of attendance. Depending on your need, you may be eligible for a subsidized loan in which the government pays the interest that accrues while you are enrolled at least half time. If you cannot demonstrate sufficient financial need according to government criteria, you may still be able to borrow, but your Stafford loan will be unsubsidized. This means that interest will accrue on the loan while you are still in school unless you arrange to pay it during this period.

In both types of Stafford loans, repayment of the principal as well as future interest begins six months after you are last enrolled on at least a half-time basis. Undergraduates may borrow a maximum of $6,625 to $10,500 per year. Graduate students may borrow up to $18,500 per year up to a maximum of $138,500, which includes any undergraduate loans you may still have. The interest rate varies annually and is set each July. Right now it is capped at 8.25 percent.

Perkins Loan Program. Another source of federal funds is the Perkins Loan program. The Perkins Loan is available to both undergraduate and graduate students who demonstrate exceptional financial need, whether enrolled full-time or part-time, and it is administered by each individual college or university. In some cases, schools reserve Perkins Loans for undergraduates. If you are an undergraduate eligible for a Perkins Loan, you may be able to borrow up to $4,000 per year with a $20,000 maximum. An eligible graduate student may be able to borrow up to $6,000 per year with a $40,000 maximum including undergraduate and graduate Perkins borrowing.

At present, the interest rate is 5 percent, and no interest accrues while you are enrolled in school at least half-time. You must start repaying the loan nine months after you are last enrolled on a half-time basis. This loan is the best deal offered by the government.

Repaying Your Federal Loans

After you graduate, leave school, or drop below half-time status, you will have a grace period of either six or nine months before loan payments start. During the grace period, you will be sent information about payment plans and your first payment due date. You can repay the loan over a maximum of 10 years with a $50 minimum monthly payment, with a graduated plan in which the payments start out low and gradually increase, or with a plan that bases your payments on your income level.

You can also consolidate all your outstanding federal loans into one loan. Having one loan to repay will minimize the chances of administrative error and allow you to write one check per month rather than several.

If you have trouble repaying your federal loans, you may qualify for a deferment or forbearance on your loan. During a deferment, payments are suspended, and if the loan is subsidized, interest does not accrue. During forbearance, payments are postponed or reduced. Repayment assistance may be available if you serve in the military.

STATE AID PROGRAMS

Some states offer financial aid to state residents that attend school in-state, some offer aid to state residents that attend school in-state or elsewhere, and some offer aid to students that attend school in their state regardless of their residency status. Some states, like California, New York, Michigan, Oklahoma, and Texas, have large aid programs. Other states may have little or nothing to offer. Contact your state scholarship office directly to find out what's available and whether you are eligible to apply. Telephone numbers are listed in the Appendix.

Private Sources of Financial Aid

In addition to the federal government, other organizations provide financial aid to students. These include your school, national and local organizations, private lenders, employers, internships, and cooperative education programs.

The College or University

Second only to the federal government in the amount of financial aid disbursed yearly are colleges and universities. Many of these institutions award both need-based and merit-based aid to deserving students. To find out more about the types of aid that the school you are interested in disburses, contact the financial aid office.

National and Local Organizations

Foundations, nonprofit organizations, churches, service and fraternal organizations, professional associations, corporations, unions, and many other national and local organizations award grants to students of higher education. Many of these awards go to students who fit a certain profile, but many of them are open to anyone who applies. The drawback of this type of aid is that you have to locate it and apply on your own.

Colleges and universities are second only to the federal government in the amount of aid they award yearly.

Private Lenders

Many students borrow from private lenders, whether through alternative loan programs, home equity loans, or other types of loans.

Alternative Loan Programs. In addition to the federal loan programs, there are many private alternative loan programs designed to help students. Most private loan programs disburse funds based on your creditworthiness rather than your financial need. Some loan programs target all types of students; others are designed specifically for graduate or professional students. In addition, you can use other types of private loans not specifically designed for education to help finance your degree. For more information, check with your bank and your school's financial aid office.

Home Equity Loans. For students who own their own homes, a home equity loan or line of credit can be an attractive financing alternative to private loan programs. Some of these loans are offered at low rates and allow you to defer payment of the principal for years. In addition, if you use the loan to pay for educational expenses, the interest on the loan is tax deductible.

Credit Cards. Whatever you do, do not use your credit cards to borrow money for school on a long-term basis. The interest rates and finance charges will be high, and the balance will grow astronomically. Credit cards are useful to pay tuition and fees if you (1) can pay the balance in full, (2) expect a student loan to come through shortly, (3) expect your employer to reimburse your costs. Otherwise, avoid them.

Internships and Cooperative Education Programs

In addition to the federal work-study program, there are other employment opportunities that may help you finance your education. Internships with organizations outside the university can provide money as well as practical experience in your field. As an intern, you are usually paid by the outside organization, and you may or may not get credit for the work you do. Although they have been common in the professional programs, such as design and business, for years, lately internships have been growing in popularity in academic programs as well.

In cooperative education programs, you usually alternate periods of full-time work in your field with periods of full-time study. You are paid for the work you do, and you may or may not get academic credit for it as well.

Internship and cooperative education programs may be administered in your department or by a separate office, so you will have to ask to find out.

Employer Reimbursement

If you work full-time and attend school part-time, you may be reimbursed for part or all of your tuition by your employer. Many employers require that you receive a minimum grade in order to qualify for reimbursement. Keep in mind, however, that your employer will withhold taxes and other deductions when it reimburses you, and you will have to make up the difference. Check with your employer before you enroll; some employers reimburse tuition only for job-related courses. Others will not reimburse employees for distance learning courses.

Some large corporations that consider job-related certificate and degrees as forms of employee training may underwrite the entire cost of a program. For example, AT&T pays Denise Petrosino's tuition directly to the University of Phoenix Online. "As long as I maintain a B average, I have 100 percent coverage," explains Petrosino, who is earning a master's degree in organizational management.

LOCATING INFORMATION ABOUT FINANCIAL AID

Finding information about financial aid can be a challenge. There is no one central clearinghouse for information about financial aid for undergraduate and graduate study. You are going to have to check a number of different sources to get the full picture on possible sources of aid that is available for you. We'll discuss a few of them here, but for a list of financial aid resources, see the Appendix.

The Government

The best source of information on federal aid for students is the U.S. government itself. The federal aid programs are administered by the U.S. Department of Education. You can contact them through their Web site, by telephone, or by mail. (See the Appendix for specifics.) Remember, however, that not all colleges and universities participate in each federal program, so if a particular federal aid program interests you, you will have to contact your school's financial aid office to make sure it's available.

If you are a graduate student, you should note that many agencies of the federal government offer fellowships to graduate students in related fields. Contact the agencies that are relevant to your field of study for further information.

For information on state aid, contact your state agency of higher education (see the Appendix).

The College or University

At a small college, the financial aid office is usually the source of all financial aid information. However, at a university, there is more than one office involved with student aid, and thus more than one source of information about it. Each university has a different administrative structure, so you will have to figure out the offices you will most likely need to contact. These may include:

- **The financial aid office.** The university-wide financial aid office is generally the best source of information about federal and private loan programs as well as university-based grants and federal work-study assistance. They may also be able to steer you to other sources of information.

- **The college or school's administrative office.** The next place to check is the administrative office of the college or school to which you are applying. For example, you may be applying for a master's degree in special education. This department may be under the jurisdiction of the College of Education. That office may or may not administer grants to the students of the college. Call to find out.

- **The office of the graduate school.** If you are a graduate student, it pays to check this administrative office; it may or may not have funding to award. If it does, the fellowships or grants are likely to be awarded on a university-wide, competitive basis.

- **The specific program or department to which you are applying.** Often a program brochure describes the types of aid that the department awards its students. If you cannot find this information in the materials you have, then call the program and ask. You'll be able to find out about program aid from this source.

It's important to check with all these offices to see what's available. It's also important to be proactive and call the financial aid office as well as other offices to find out your chances of receiving aid.

The Internet

The Internet is an excellent source of information about all types of financial aid. One of the best places to start your Internet search for financial aid is the Financial Aid Information Page at www.finaid.org. This site has a great deal of information about the different types of financial aid and provides links to other relevant sites as well. It provides a good overview of the financial aid situation. In addition, the site offers several calculators that enable you to estimate many useful figures, including your Estimated Family Contribution, projected costs of attendance, and future student loan payments. There are also a number of searchable databases of national scholarships and fellow-ships on the Internet. One searchable database of financial aid resources can be found on Peterson's Web site (www.petersons.com/resources/finance.html). Another scholarship database is FastWeb at www.fastweb.com. On each of these sites, you'll need to answer a questionnaire about your educational background, field of study, and personal characteristics. When you are done, the database is searched to match your data with eligibility requirements of several hundred thousand fellowships and scholarships. You are then given a list of possible fellowships and scholarships to pursue on your own. There is no cost for either of these services.

One of the best places to start an Internet search for financial aid information is the Financial Aid Information Page at www.finaid.org.

There are a few things you should beware of when using Internet search services. First, a searchable database is only as good as its index, so you may find yourself getting some odd matches. In addition, most searchable databases of scholarships and fellowships are designed primarily for undergraduates, so the number of potential matches for a graduate student is far fewer than the several hundred thousand sources of aid that a database may contain. Finally, some of these Internet search services charge a fee. Given the amount of free information that's available, both on the Internet and in libraries, it's not necessary to pay for this type of research.

Print Directories

Although the searchable databases on the Internet are easy to use, it's still a good idea to check print directories of national scholarships, grants, and fellowships. These directories have indexes that make locating potential sources of funds easy. Scholarships, grants, and fellowships are indexed by field of study as well as by type of student. So, for example, you can search for all funding related to the study of Latin America or electrical engineering. Or you can search for funding that is targeted to Hispanic students, disabled students, or adult students. It's a good idea just to browse, too, in case something catches your eye.

There are quite a few directories that you can consult. For undergraduates, Peterson's *Scholarships, Grants, & Prizes 2001* lists many private sources of aid, and Peterson's *College Money Handbook 2001* covers college and university sources of financial aid. For graduate students, the *Annual Register of Grant Support: A Directory of Funding Sources*, published by the National Register Publishing Company, is a comprehensive guide to awards from the government, foundations, and business and professional organizations.

APPLYING FOR FINANCIAL AID

Depending on your personal situation and the requirements of the school, you may have to submit just one or a number of applications for financial aid. If you apply for need-based aid, university merit aid, national scholarships and fellowships, or private loan programs, you will have several application forms to deal with. However many applications you must submit, start the process early.

Deadlines

"I cannot overemphasize the importance of applying early," says Emerelle McNair, director of scholarships and financial aid at Southern Polytechnic State University in Georgia. "Most awards are made in spring for the following academic year." Be sure you've picked the correct deadlines from your program application information packet.

Students applying for financial aid often have an earlier deadline for the entire application. If you look for sources of aid outside the program and university, such as national scholarships and fellowships, then it is even more important to start your research early—a full year or more before you plan to enroll.

Remember, it can easily take months to fill out applications and assemble all the supporting data for a financial aid request. You may need to submit income tax forms, untaxed income verification, asset verification, and documents that support any special circumstances you are claiming. For private scholarship applications, you may need to write an essay and provide letters of recommendation. So give yourself plenty of time to submit the initial application. Later, if you are asked to provide additional information or supporting documents, do so as quickly as possible.

The FAFSA

The Free Application for Federal Student Aid (FAFSA) is the only form you will need to apply for most federal need-based aid programs and state aid programs as well. FAFSA is used by both undergraduate and graduate students. The FAFSA form is issued annually by the Department of Education at the end of each calendar year (see www.fafsa.ed. gov), and it is available both in paper and on line. You use it to report financial data from the previous year in order to be considered for aid in the school year that starts the following fall. It's much easier to fill out the FAFSA if you have already done your federal income tax forms for the year, but since most schools require you to file the FAFSA in January or February, that may be difficult. If your federal income tax return is not done, use estimates so you can file the FAFSA on time. You can amend it later if necessary. Because the FAFSA is designed for undergraduate students who are dependent on their parents, if you are a working adult student you may find you are having difficulty interpreting some of the questions or that the questions do not cover all your circumstances. If there is information about your financial situation that is not elicited by the FAFSA but that you feel is germane to your application, then explain the circumstances in a separate letter to the financial aid office of the schools to which you apply. Suppose, for

Whatever you do, don't miss financial aid application deadlines.

If your federal income tax return is not done, use estimates so you can file the FAFSA on time.

example, that you have been working full-time for a few years but you are planning to quit your job and attend school full-time. You would complete the FAFSA using the previous year's full-time income figures, but this would not be an accurate reflection of your financial situation during the following school year because your income will drop precipitously. In such a case, you would notify the financial aid office so that it can make a professional judgment as to whether or not your need should be revised upward.

After you submit the FAFSA, you will receive a Student Aid Report (SAR), an acknowledgment that includes a summary of the data you have sent them. Check to make sure the information is accurate and that the schools you have chosen to have the data sent to are correctly listed. If there are errors, make corrections right away. The SAR will also show your Expected Family Contribution, the amount you and your spouse (or parents if you are still a dependent) will be expected to contribute. This information is used by each school to calculate your financial need (cost of attendance minus Expected Family Contribution) and to award need-based aid.

School's Financial Aid Application Form or CSS PROFILE

A school may require that you submit a separate financial aid application in addition to the program application and the FAFSA. If you do not see such a form in the program application packet, call the admissions office to find out whether or not you need to obtain it from another office.

Some schools do not have their own financial aid application form. Instead, they require you to submit a standardized form, the College Scholarship Service's (CSS) Financial Aid PROFILE. This form is similar to the FAFSA, but it is used to award university aid.

The Program Application

For many schools, the program application is the main application for university-based aid. Much of the nonfederal university-based aid for incoming students is determined by the admissions committee's assessment of the merit of program applications. So a strong program application, submitted on time, will improve your chances of getting aid from the program or university. Since you cannot predict which elements of your application will be weighted most heavily by a given admissions committee, do your best on all of them.

National and Private Scholarship and Fellowship Applications

If you apply for national and/or private scholarships and fellowships, you will have to submit separate applications for each one to the awarding organizations. Follow instructions carefully, making sure you meet all deadlines. Some scholarship applications can be as elaborate as program applications, with letters of recommendation and essays, so allow yourself a lot of time to complete them.

Following Up

Just as you do with your program application, follow up with your financial aid applications as well. If you do not receive the SAR, an acknowledgment that your FAFSA form was received, within a few weeks of filing the FAFSA, check on its status. In addition, call the university offices with which you are dealing to make sure everything is proceeding smoothly.

TAX BENEFITS FOR STUDENTS

Whether or not you receive financial aid, there are many recently enacted tax benefits for adults who want to return to school (as well as for parents who send or plan to send their children to college). In effect, these tax cuts make the first two years of college universally available, and they give many more working adults the financial means to go back to school. About 12.9 million students benefit—5.8 million under the HOPE Scholarship tax credit and 7.1 million under the Lifetime Learning tax credit. Countless others benefit from new rules concerning Individual Retirement Accounts (IRAs) and state tuition savings plans as well as from deductions on student loan interest and employer reimbursements for education expenses.

The HOPE Scholarship Tax Credit

The HOPE Scholarship tax credit helps make the first two years of college or career school more affordable. Students whose adjusted gross income falls within certain limits receive a 100 percent tax credit for the first $1,000 of tuition and required fees and a 50 percent credit on the second $1,000. This credit is available for tuition and required fees less grants, scholarships, and other tax-free educational assistance. The credit is phased out for joint filers whose adjusted gross income is between $80,000 and $100,000 and for single filers whose adjusted gross income is between $40,000 and $50,000.

The HOPE Scholarship tax credit can be claimed for students who are in their first two years of college or career school and who are enrolled on at least a half-time basis in a degree or certificate program for any portion of the year. The taxpayer can claim a credit for his own tuition expense or for the expenses of his or her spouse or dependent children.

The Lifetime Learning Tax Credit

The Lifetime Learning tax credit is targeted toward adults who want to go back to school, change careers, or take a course or two to upgrade their skills as well as to college juniors, seniors, and graduate and professional degree students. A family may receive a 20 percent tax credit for the first $5,000 of tuition and required fees paid each year through 2002, and for the first $10,000 thereafter.

Just like the HOPE Scholarship tax credit, the Lifetime Learning tax credit is available for tuition and required fees less grants, scholarships, and other tax-free educational assistance. The maximum credit is determined on a per-taxpayer (family) basis, regardless of the number of postsecondary students in the family, and it is phased out at the same income levels as the HOPE Scholarship tax credit. Families can claim the Lifetime Learning tax credit for some members of their family and the HOPE Scholarship tax credit for others who qualify in the same year.

Individual Retirement Accounts

Since January 1, 1998, taxpayers have been able to withdraw funds from an IRA, without penalty, for their own higher education expenses or those of their spouse, child, or even grandchild. However, you do have to pay income taxes on the amount you withdraw.

In addition, for each child under age 18, families may deposit $500 per year into an education IRA in the child's name. Earnings in the education IRA accumulate tax-free, and no taxes are due upon withdrawal if the money is used to pay for postsecondary tuition and required fees (less grants, scholarships, and other tax-free educational assistance), books, equipment, and eligible room and board expenses. Once the child reaches age 30, his or her education IRA must be closed or transferred to a younger member of the family.

A taxpayer's ability to contribute to an education IRA is phased out when the taxpayer is a joint filer with an adjusted gross income between $150,000 and $160,000, or a single filer with an adjusted gross income between $95,000 and $110,000. There are a few restrictions. For example, a student who receives the tax-free distributions from an education IRA may not, in the same year, benefit from the HOPE Scholarship or Lifetime Learning tax credits.

State Tuition Plans

When a family uses a qualified state-sponsored tuition plan to save for college, no tax is due in connection with the plan until the time of withdrawal. Families can now use these plans to save not only for tuition but also for certain room and board expenses for students who attend college on at least a half-time basis. Tuition and required fees paid with withdrawals from a qualified state tuition plan are eligible for the HOPE Scholarship tax credit and Lifetime Learning tax credit.

Tax-Deductible Student Loan Interest

For many graduates, one of the first financial obligations is to repay their student loans. The new student loan interest deduction reduces the burden of the repayment obligation by allowing students or their families to take a tax deduction for interest paid in the first 60 months of repayment on student loans. The deduction is available even if an individual does not itemize other deductions.

The maximum deduction of $2,000 in 2000 rises to $2,500 in 2001 and beyond. It is phased out for joint filers with adjusted gross income between $60,000 and $75,000, and for single filers with adjusted gross income between $40,000 and $55,000.

Tax-Deductible Employer Reimbursements

If you take undergraduate courses and your employer reimburses you for education-related expenses, you may be able to exclude up to $5,250 of employer-provided education benefits from your income. Reimbursement for graduate and professional courses is not eligible for this exclusion and is counted as taxable income.

Community Service Loan Forgiveness

This provision excludes from your income any student loan amounts forgiven by nonprofit, tax-exempt charitable, or educational institutions for borrowers who take community-service jobs that address unmet community needs. For example, a recent graduate who takes a low-paying job in a rural school will not owe any additional income tax if in recognition of this service her college or another charity forgives a loan it made to her to help pay her college costs. This provision applies to loans forgiven after August 5, 1997.

For Additional Information

The tax issues relating to higher education are discussed in more detail in Internal Revenue Service Publication 970, *Tax Benefits for Higher Education*. To obtain a copy, visit the Internal Revenue Service Web site at www.irs.gov or call 800-829-3676 (toll-free).

PAYING FOR SCHOOL IS POSSIBLE

You can see that it *is* possible to find the financial aid that will help you pay for school. You will have to be persistent in your search for funds. You may have to spend time working on financial aid research and applications. You may have to borrow money. And once you enter a program, you may have to simplify your lifestyle in order to cut your expenses.

But if you really want to earn a degree or certificate, you can find the financial help that will make it possible. Be realistic about your needs, leave yourself enough time to complete all the paperwork, and do your homework. Now is a good time to look back on all the reasons why you want to continue your education—to remind yourself why it's worth it.

Succeeding as a Distance Learner

Chapter 9

Congratulations! You have weathered the selection and application process and you are about to embark on a new phase of your education. As you will soon find out for yourself, taking courses at a distance is not like going to class on campus. Distance learners often have the convenience of setting their own hours and pacing themselves in their studies. As we have seen in previous chapters, the instructional technology lends itself to innovative approaches to teaching and learning, including more student participation and collaboration, especially in online courses. You'll find that because you work at a distance you will have more time to reflect about and respond to what you learn as well as to take part in discussions. You may be surprised at the ways in which the community of learning develops in a well-run distance course.

Of course, distance learners face a few challenges unique to the instructional design of distance courses. As a distance learner, you'll be expected to organize your time, work independently as well as collaboratively, take the initiative in your studies, and monitor your own progress, all while mastering the technology and using it as a valuable tool for learning.

So, in addition to the basic study skills you would need to earn any degree—reading, writing, analytical thinking, and test-taking skills— you will need other skills and strategies to succeed at distance learning. In this chapter we'll give you some suggestions and tips from successful distance learners that will help you become a more effective and successful student yourself.

MASTERING THE TECHNOLOGY

We'll start with technology, because success in distance learning depends first upon reliable technology that you understand how to use. Once you've mastered the technology, it will recede into the background and become something you simply use and even take for granted.

Having the Right Equipment

Before you start a course, make sure you have the technological tools you will need to participate in discussions and complete assignments. Most programs provide a list of technical requirements ahead of time. If your course is on line, get a list of the hardware and software required, and make sure the computer you plan to use is properly equipped and that you have a reliable Internet service provider. If you take a course via broadcast or videotapes, learn how to use your VCR. If you have to buy equipment, don't skimp on specifications to save a few dollars now. The money you spend now to make sure you have the appropriate hardware and software is money well spent, because you'll find it much easier to get your work done properly if you are not struggling with inadequate machinery.

Improving Your Technology Skills

If you have the proper equipment but think you may not be up to speed technologically, try to improve your technology skills before courses start. As we discussed in Chapter 5, many colleges offer online tutorials or sample minicourses that you can take if you feel you need some practice with the technology before you actually take your first course. "I am a computer novice and never realized the extent of the computer's online capabilities until I had to learn about it through trial and error," reports a language arts literacy teacher who took a graduate course on line from Rutgers University. "This was very frustrating." So if you have the opportunity for a sample course or practice session before courses begin, take it.

Tips for Succeeding with Technology

To master the technology involved in your distance courses:

- Make sure you have the appropriate hardware and software for your courses, and don't skimp on the specifications if you need to purchase any items.

- Take a tutorial or sample minicourse ahead of time to familiarize yourself with the instructional technology.
- Allow yourself extra time at the beginning of the course to navigate the technology.
- Keep copies of your assignments and back up your computer files.
- Ask for help when you need it. Well-run distance programs have technological support via telephone seven days a week, 24 hours a day.

Remember, the technology involved in distance learning is a tool that anyone can master—it just may take some effort.

LEARNING ABOUT LIBRARY RESOURCES

Once you've got the technology working for you, the next resource you need to familiarize yourself with is the library. Understanding how to use a library is important to any student's success, but it is especially important for distance students who may not be able to get to a good bricks-and-mortar university library to get the materials they need.

Taking an Orientation Program

One of the first things you should check before courses begin is whether or not a library services orientation program designed for distance students is available. If it is, sign up to take the orientation right away. "An early orientation to library resources, particularly interlibrary loans, is needed for those who can't physically access a library," recommends Kurt Krause, a hotel manager who took an online hospitality management course from Virginia Tech. Learning about library services through an orientation program will save you time later on when you actually need to do research for a course.

Learning What's Available On Line

Although the Internet has revolutionized the way we look for and store information, don't make the mistake of thinking that all the information you will need is available on the Internet. True, many journals, databases, catalogs, and newspapers are instantaneously available on

"An early orientation to library resources, particularly interlibrary loans, is needed for those who can't physically access a library," suggests Kurt Krause.

line, and you can access them directly or through the university library if a subscription is needed. However, the material that's available on line is only a fraction of the total resources of a library. Books, for example, are still primarily in print form. Many academic journals provide only abstracts (not full-text articles) on line, and a few are not on line at all. Reference services may be available only face-to-face or by telephone. And reserve collections may or may not be available on line. So one of the first tasks you face is to learn just what you can access on line via the university library or directly on the Internet and what you must access in paper, microform, or other physical media.

Planning Ahead to Get the Materials You Need

The reason you will need to know what your research resources are fairly early in the game is that you will have to plan ahead if you need to access nondigitized (paper) information at a distance, especially if the material needs to be secured via interlibrary loan. "Because I did not have physical access to a medical library in my community, I had to organize my data collection for assigned papers early in the semester," explains Patti Iversen. "The biggest handicap was the time delay in ordering and receiving full-text articles. A time lapse of three weeks from time of request to delivery of articles was common." You can see the need to plan ahead under these circumstances.

Tips for Succeeding with Library Resources

In order to be prepared for course work, early in the term or, even better, before the term starts:

- **Take a library orientation if one if available.** If there is no formal distance orientation, call the library and ask for an informal orientation.
- **Check your local public and university libraries.** Find out what resources they have and whether or not you can arrange access.
- **Check each course syllabus very early in the term.** Determine whether you can obtain everything you will need on line or whether you will have to make other arrangements for some items.

- **Use the reference services of your university library.** Ask for help. Reference librarians are there to help you, even if it's by e-mail or over the phone.

MANAGING YOUR TIME

"If you are a student at any college, there is one thing you just don't have enough of....TIME! Everything is about time," says Cena Barber, an undergraduate who has taken online courses toward her degree in political science and history at Drake University in Iowa. For students who have family and work responsibilities as well, lack of time is a particularly acute problem. "With life's challenges, kids, family, job—it's hard to keep your studies a high priority," explains Scott Garrod, who is earning a master's degree in business from Syracuse University. "When your four-year-old wants a story read, do you have to study your accounting? That's an easy choice, but it means making up the accounting at a later time."

General Tips for Managing Your Time

Not having enough time is a common problem. Distance learners can approach this problem in several ways:

- **Be realistic about how many courses you can handle.** If you work and/or have a family, you will have relatively little time to spend on schoolwork. Start out with one or two courses at a time, and then if you feel you can increase your courseload, do so. This is especially important if you take a distance course for the first time and don't know exactly what to expect.

- **Set up a regular time to study, but expect to be interrupted.** If you have a study schedule, you are more likely to get your schoolwork done, but be sure to leave some extra time. Unless you live alone, you'll need time for your family commitments. Young kids, especially, don't much care what you are doing when they need a parent, so if possible try to schedule study time when they are not around.

"With life's challenges, kids, family, job—it's hard to keep your studies a high priority," says distance student Scott Garrod.

- **Set up a regular place to study.** Although it may be difficult if you are doing schoolwork at home, try to establish a study area that's yours alone to use. If possible, the area should be quiet and free of distractions. "Since you are doing the work at home you can be easily distracted," explains Andrea Bessel, who is earning a bachelor's degree in business administration from the State University of New York at Oswego. "A lot of times something comes up and I end up setting my homework aside, which is not a good habit to get into." So if necessary, do schoolwork at your local public library or from work if your employer permits it.

- **Set priorities on what you have to do.** Make judgments about what you need to do, and then spend your time on activities that are the most important and must be done first. Get used to the fact that you may have to postpone some tasks.

- **Set deadlines.** Distance learning can be very unstructured, so you probably will have to be your own taskmaster. "I have learned that I have to set deadlines for myself," says Brigit Dolan, who is earning a master's degree from Gonzaga University in Washington, "or I will never get anything done."

- **Don't procrastinate.** "Procrastination is your worst enemy," claims Robin Barnes, who earned a master's degree in nursing (family nurse-practitioner) from Gonzaga University.

- **Use time-management tools to help you schedule your time.** Planners, whether paper or electronic, can help you allocate time and keep track of deadlines. "To do" lists can help you manage your short-term commitments.

"I have learned that I have to set deadlines for myself," says Brigit Dolan, "or I will never get anything done."

MANAGING TIME IN ONLINE COURSES

In addition to the lack of time that all students contend with, online distance learners face unique challenges associated with time, namely, managing the flexibility of the online format and dealing with lag time when communicating with students and faculty members.

Game Plan for Distance Learning

Managing the Flexibility of Online Courses

Flexibility is a unique advantage that attracts people to asynchronous courses, especially online courses. But flexibility can have a downside as well. "The best thing about distance learning is the freedom to set one's own hours for study and learning. The worst thing about distance learning is the freedom to set one's own hours for study and learning!" exclaims a middle school language arts literacy teacher taking an online graduate course from Rutgers. "Although it hasn't happened to me, it is easy to put aside work and projects for the course when one is not locked into a regular schedule. I can see how one could easily fall behind through a lack of discipline." So you can see that you'll have to use your time-management skills to take advantage of the flexibility and not let it take advantage of you.

Managing the Amount of Time Spent On Line

Not only does the flexibility of online courses mean that you need discipline to log on regularly, but once you are connected you have, in theory, as much time as you want to spend on the course. Cena Barber points out, "There is no time limit as to how long the class lasts. It could be five minutes one day and five hours the next." Unless you are careful, it's easy to spend more time than you really have on an online course, so before you log on, decide how much time you have to spend during that session.

Getting Accustomed to the Pace

Another difference between online and traditional courses that comes as a surprise to many students is the pace at which discussions proceed. In an online course, there is a time interval between when you post a message and when you get a response—in an asynchronous discussion group—or when you send an e-mail and get a reply. Hours, even days, may elapse between exchanges on a topic, and it can take a while to get used to the slow progress of communication.

The time delay sometimes becomes a problem when students work on a group project with deadlines. "Given the time lag, it took ever so much more time to get anything done if you had to collaborate with anyone," explains a library media specialist taking an online

> **"The best thing about distance learning is the freedom to set one's own hours for study and learning. The worst thing about distance learning is the freedom to set one's own hours for study and learning!"**

postgraduate course from Rutgers. "When would they open the discussion thread? When would they respond? These were frustrations that I hadn't counted on and found difficult to deal with." To solve these problems, groups working on projects often communicate by telephone or in real-time chat rooms.

Tips for Managing Time in Online Courses

Given the asynchronous nature of online courses, you will not be able to completely solve the time problems they pose. However, you can minimize or avoid them to some degree.

- **Set a schedule for logging on.** Even though no one may have given you a daily class schedule, you will benefit if you work one out for yourself. "You should become accustomed to getting on line on a regular basis," advises Vania McBean, a computer studies major at University of Maryland University College. "I log on each day to see what is new."
- **Limit the amount of time you will spend on line at one session.** The limit might be 1 hour, for example. On some days that will be too much time, and on others, too little, but at least you will have a benchmark to aim for.
- **Don't fret about the time delays in asynchronous discussions.** Before you know it, you will have become used to this method of communication and it will no longer seem odd.
- **Use a chat room or the telephone when asynchronous communication becomes too slow.** You can make an appointment to meet in a chat room or have a teleconference if group work needs to be accomplished more efficiently. If e-mailing a fellow student or the instructor takes too long, try telephoning.

"You should become accustomed to getting on line on a regular basis," advises Vania McBean. "I log on each day to see what is new."

MANAGING TIME IN VIDEOTAPED COURSES

Students that take courses in which on-campus lectures are videotaped and mailed to them face a different set of time-management challenges. First, the weekly videotapes may take a considerable amount of time to watch. And second, the taping, duplicating, and delivery time means that distance students lag behind on-campus students in the same course.

Scheduling Time to Watch the Videos

Depending on the course load, students that take videotaped courses may find themselves with 3 to 12 hours or more of videotape to watch each week on top of their assignments. Essentially, the amount of time is the same as it would be if they had to attend classes. Since they don't have to attend classes, inexperienced students may put off watching the videos, thinking they can catch up at a later date. "In the first semester, the learning curve is steep," comments Dale Ann Abendroth, assistant professor of nursing at Gonzaga University. "So I set up my assignments to force students into a pattern of watching the videotapes." If you have a savvy instructor, the assignments will put you on a schedule. If the instructor doesn't take a structured approach, you will need to plan a regular schedule to watch the videos in order to keep up with the course work.

Managing the Delay between Distance and On-Campus Students

In videotaped courses, the distance students are a half-week to a week behind the on-campus students. "It can get a little confusing when reading topics don't correspond with lecture topics because the tapes arrive one week later than the class," explains Carla Gentry, who is earning a Master of Science in Nursing (family nurse practitioner) from Gonzaga University. If the course also has a Web-based component, the distance students have to cope with joining the Web-based discussion group and receiving the readings before the videotaped lectures arrive.

Schools do try to solve this time-delay problem, with mixed success. "Throughout the semester, we have a one-week lag on assignment due dates (in comparison to the students who are actually in class on campus)," explains Nicole DeRaleau, who is earning a master's degree in engineering from Worcester Polytechnic Institute in Massachusetts. "At the end of the semester, however, we have a one-week disadvantage because the whole class has to turn in final assignments, projects, and finals on the same date in order to get grades done on time," says DeRaleau. "This can be *very* stressful." In contrast, at Gonzaga University's nursing program, distance students are permitted to take their final exams in their local communities a few days later than the on-campus students. "These are logistical problems that both the faculty and students become accustomed to solving," explains Abendroth.

Tips for Managing Time in Videotaped Courses

There are a couple of things you can do to manage your time if you take videotaped courses:

- **Set a schedule for watching the videotapes.** Even though you don't have to show up for class, you still need to put in classroom time in front of your own TV. If you're good at multitasking, you can follow Brigit Dolan's lead. "Sometimes I'm able to pick up my house while listening and taking in the information," explains the graduate student.
- **Keep up with your course work.** Since at times you may need to complete assignments or take exams with less lead time than on-campus students have, it's imperative that you keep up with the work on a regular basis. You may face an end-of-term time crunch, so study regularly throughout the course to minimize its effect.

COMMUNICATING WITH FACULTY

When you are a distance learner you can't just raise your hand and ask a question or stay after class to talk with the instructor. Even in two-way interactive video classes, which are more similar to traditional classes than other distance learning formats, there can be difficulties in communicating with an instructor at a remote location. "It can be a little more inconvenient to speak with your instructor if you need to ask about something you wouldn't ask in front of the whole class," reports a horticulture student taking a two-way interactive video course from the University of Cincinnati.

"Sometimes you do more self-teaching because you cannot just drop into the instructor's office."

For students in online and videotaped courses, communicating with an instructor can be slow. "Sometimes you do more self-teaching because you cannot just drop into the instructor's office," explains Robin Barnes. "You may have to wait a day or two for an answer to a question. Have patience and be kind to yourself." However, you can use technology to your advantage in communicating with faculty members. E-mail, for example, is an excellent way to contact a faculty member to find out what his or her expectations are, to clarify assignments, or simply to ask a question. You may not get a response immediately, but most faculty members will answer their e-mail within a day or two. In fact, you should make a point of communicating with your instructor in distance courses. "Be sure to communicate regularly with your professor because [the course] can seem pretty far removed if you are not getting feedback every week or so," advises Sonja Cole, a middle school media specialist taking online courses from Rutgers.

Tips for Communicating with Faculty Members

To ensure you get the input an instructor can provide and to make yourself known, here are some strategies for communicating with faculty members:

- **Participate in online discussion groups.** Although your instructor may not comment all the time, he or she is following the class's discussions and will get to know you there.
- **Participate in class discussions in two-way interactive video courses.** It's easy to "hide in the back of the class" if you attend a course in a remote location, but you'll get more out of the class if you respond to the instructor and the class discussion.
- **Be assertive in communicating with your instructors.** "You have to take the initiative," advises a distance learning student. "If you do not make sure that you get the best learning opportunity that you can, no one is going to do that for you." Remember, most faculty members are more than happy to help their students.
- **Use e-mail or the telephone.** If you need to communicate with the instructor privately, use e-mail or the telephone. Most faculty members will respond within a day or two.

"You have to take the initiative," advises a distance learning student. **"If you do not make sure that you get the best learning opportunity that you can, no one is going to do that for you."**

REACHING OUT TO YOUR FELLOW STUDENTS

Just as you should take the initiative in communicating with your instructors, you should also be proactive in communicating with fellow students. Communicating with your peers has two benefits: it helps you feel connected to the learning community and it enables you to learn from your fellow students. In addition, establishing good communication with fellow students is key to successful collaborative efforts.

Making Connections with the Learning Community

"I have made a conscious effort to build relationships with other students and to keep e-mail contact with them," explains Patti Iversen, a graduate student who lives in Montana and takes distance courses from Gonzaga University in Washington. "This allows each of us the opportunity to get feedback and commiserate." Another student, who is earning a bachelor's degree in information systems management from University of Maryland University College, reports, "My experience with fellow classmates in the online classroom has been very positive. I have found that establishing relationships, despite the fact that they are short-lived, has aided me." During periods when your motivation flags, this connection with others in your courses can help energize you and put you back on track.

"I have made a conscious effort to build relationships with other students and to keep e-mail contact with them," says Patti Iversen.

Taking Advantage of What Your Peers Have to Offer

Second, your fellow students can be resources for you. Many distance students are adults with considerable life and professional experience, so they can contribute as much as they learn from the interactions in a course. According to Michael Olsen, who teaches distance courses on the hospitality industry at Virginia Tech, students in his courses "are mature, industry-experienced professionals who come extremely well prepared. They are good contributors and they are not afraid to interact." Scott Garrod, who is pursuing a master's degree in business from Syracuse University, likes the broad range of people he meets through his distance courses. "You do not develop deep relationships," he explains, "but in a distance program you meet a wider range of individuals across multiple countries and careers."

Since all this knowledge and experience is within easy reach, you should take advantage of it. "You need to read through the responses that others post on the Web, so that you actually gain something from the forum discussion," explains Beth Grote, a Drake University student who took a course on line. Some students do more than simply participate in class and in online discussion groups—they form study groups of their own. "You just have to make it a point to form an Internet study group," suggests Robin Barnes. "We would try to converse once a week, more often if we were working on a project."

Working on Group Projects

Since instructors often assign group projects in distance courses to help forge a community of learners, you will probably find yourself working with others much more frequently than you did in your past on-campus classes. According to several distance students we surveyed, doing group projects well is one of the most challenging aspects of distance learning. Often the logistics of getting a group of busy working adults in different time zones to meet at an appointed time in a chat room or be available for a conference call can be daunting. In some online courses, separate discussion groups are formed so group members can communicate asynchronously. "You need to have lots of patience and dedication," warns Kevin Ruthen, who earned a master's degree in information resource management from Syracuse University. "Interaction in an online environment can often be more time-consuming than an on-campus meeting."

And the problems of interaction are not limited to time factors. In the online environment, it's sometimes difficult for a group to coalesce and assign roles and tasks to its members. "In one of my courses, members tiptoed around each other, no one wanting to seem overbearing and declare themselves the leader, boss, facilitator, whatever. But we really needed one," explains a library media specialist taking online courses from Rutgers. "It took quite a while for a shakedown to occur so that some work could be accomplished." She continues, "Another problem was what to do about members of the team who were unproductive. It's very hard to prod people over the Internet. On the other hand, since you don't have the opportunity for meandering, off-topic conversations that start in onsite classes, things move swiftly, on schedule."

Tips for Communicating Well with Your Peers

To make the most of your interactions with your fellow students, you can use these suggestions:

- **Participate.** You should participate in discussions, whether they are in class in two-way interactive video courses or are on line. You will get a lot more out of your courses if you take an active part. In addition, you will get to know the other students and they will get to know you.

- **Share your knowledge and experiences.** Don't assume you have nothing to offer. Most adults have plenty of experience and knowledge that can be of value to others.

- **If you need support from other students, ask for it.** Everyone runs into occasional problems in a course, even if the problem is simply feeling overwhelmed by the amount of work you have to do. Communicating with other students can help you solve problems and get back on track, or it can simply make you feel better because you've let off some steam.

- **Use various forms of communication as needed.** Don't feel limited to class time or discussion groups. You can e-mail or call people with whom you'd like to converse in private. Remember, other distance students may feel somewhat disconnected from the group, too, and they will probably welcome an overture from you.

- **Be assertive.** When you work in a group, be assertive about what you can contribute. If the group is not making progress, try to use some of your leadership skills to get things moving.

ENLISTING YOUR FAMILY'S SUPPORT

One of the main benefits of most distance learning courses is that you can take the course from home. But unless you live alone, that means that you are working from a shared space in the presence of your family. Not only do they have to cope with the fact that you have less time for them, but they have to watch you be inaccessible—not an easy task. Therefore you should make sure you enlist the support and cooperation of your family; having their support will make your life—and theirs—much easier.

One distance student has made her education something of a family enterprise. "I work full-time, and I am blessed with a wonderful, supportive husband and the two greatest children one could ever dream of," says LaVonne Johnson, who is earning a master's degree in nursing from Gonzaga University. "We are in this together, everyone helping on some level," she continues. "My husband cooks, cleans, does laundry, and will proof papers if he is the last resort. My thirteen-year-old daughter is a great help around the house and my sixteen-year-old son is always helping with Power Point projects, statistical analyses, and Excel graphs. Needless to say, in return I try really hard not to impact my family any more than they already are, and we get by."

IN CONCLUSION

Distance learning is challenging, but with motivation, self-discipline, and the support of family, coworkers, and fellow students, you can succeed in your courses and earn a certificate or degree if that's your goal. Perhaps the best summation of distance education we encountered from the scores of students we surveyed came from Patti Iversen:

"We are in this together, everyone helping on some level," distance learner LaVonne Johnson explains.

> Distance learning isn't for the faint of heart or those who require considerable reinforcement to remain on task. It is sometimes difficult for others to recognize the challenges of the distance learner, as job, family, and community activities all continue as before. Finding a way to carve out of a busy schedule the time necessary to successfully complete courses that seem relatively invisible is a big challenge. At the same time, there is absolutely no way that I could have hoped to accomplish the goal that I have set for myself except as a distance learner. I am able to stretch and grow, professionally and personally, while continuing to live a lifestyle that I value immensely. It isn't always an easy task—it is often rigorous and sometimes frustrating—but distance learning has opened a gate of opportunity for me that previously was inaccessible.

Distance learning can provide that opportunity for you as well.

RESOURCES

Chapter 1: What Is Distance Education?

You can find endless sources of information about distance education by doing an Internet search. One Web site that lists links to distance learning resources is dmoz.org/Reference/Education/Distance_Learning. Some other good sources of information include the following:

> *The Chronicle of Higher Education*
> 1255 23d Street, NW
> Washington, DC 20037
> Telephone: 202-466-1000
> E-mail: circulation@chronicle.com
> Web site: chronicle.com

> *Distance Learning in Higher Education.* Council for Higher Education Accreditation, CHEA Update No. 3, June 2000. Available at www.chea.org/Commentary/distance-learning-3.cfm

> Russell, Thomas L. *The No Significant Difference Phenomenon.* Available at cuda.teleeducation.nb.ca/nosignificantdifference/

> *Survey on Distance Education at Postsecondary Education Institutions, 1997–1998.* NCES 2000-13, by Laurie Lewis, Kyle Snow, Elizabeth Farris, Douglas Levin. Bernie Green, project officer. U.S. Department of Education, National Center for Education Statistics, Washington, DC 1999. Available on line at nces.ed.gov.

> U.S. Distance Learning Association
> 140 Gould Street
> Needham, MA 02494-2397
> Telephone: 800-275-5162 (toll-free)
> Web site: www.usdla.org

Chapter 2: Is Distance Learning Right for You?

Sometimes it helps to have some objective help when you are assessing your goals, aptitudes, strengths, and weaknesses:

> National Board for Certified Counselors

Game Plan for Distance Learning

Appendix

3 Terrace Way, Suite D
Greensboro, NC 27403-3660
Telephone: 800-398-5389 (toll-free)
E-mail: nbcc@nbcc.org
Web site: www.nbcc.org

Chapter 3: What Can You Study via Distance Learning?

Internet Databases

Peterson's: www.petersons.com/dlearn

Print Directories

Guide to Distance Learning Programs in Canada 2001. Education International, 2001.

Peterson's *MBA Distance Learning Programs 2000.* Princeton, NJ: Peterson's, 1999.

Peterson's *Guide to Distance Learning Programs 2001.* Princeton, NJ: Peterson's, 2000.

Equivalency Examinations

College Level Examination Program (CLEP)
P.O. Box 6600
Princeton, NJ 08541-6600
Telephone: 609-771-7865
E-mail: clep@info.collegeboard.org
Web site: www.collegeboard.org/clep

CLEP Success. Princeton, NJ: Peterson's, 2000.
Lieberman, Leo, et al. *CLEP.* Arco, 1999.

DANTES Subject Standardized Tests (DSSTs)
Telephone: 609-720-6740
E-mail: dantes@chauncey.com *or* exams@voled.doded.mil
Web site: www.chauncey.com/dantes *or* www.voled.doded.mil/dantes/exam

Excelsior College Examination Program (formerly Regents College Examinations)

Test Administration Office
Excelsior College
7 Columbia Circle
Albany, NY 12203-5159
Telephone: 888-647–2388 (toll-free)
E-mail: testadmn@excelsior.edu
Web site: www.excelsior.edu/100.htm

GRE Subject Area Tests
GRE-ETS
P.O. Box 6000
Princeton, NJ 08541-6000
Telephone: 609-771-7670
E-mail: gre-info@ets.org
Web site: www.gre.org

Assessment for Life Experience
Council for Adult and Experiential Learning (CAEL)
55 East Monroe Street, Suite 1930
Chicago, IL 60603
Telephone: 312-499-2600
Web site: www.cael.org

Credit for Work Training
American Council on Education
Center for Adult Learning Educational Credentials
One Dupont Circle NW
Washington, DC 20036
Telephone: 202-939-9475
E-mail: credit@ace.nche.edu
Web site: www.acenet.edu

Credit for Military Training
Servicemembers Opportunities Colleges
1307 New York Avenue NW, fifth floor
Washington, DC 20005-4701
Telephone: 800-368-5622 (toll-free)
E-mail: socmail@aascu.org
Web site: www.soc.aascu.org

Chapter 5: Selecting a Good Distance Learning Program

The names and contact information of all agencies recognized by the U.S. Department of Education (www.ed.gov/offices/OPE/accreditation/natlagencies.html) and the Council for Higher Education Accreditation (www.chea.org) are listed below.

Institutional Accrediting Agencies—Regional

Middle States Association of Colleges and Schools

Accredits institutions in Delaware, District of Columbia, Maryland, New Jersey, New York, Pennsylvania, Puerto Rico, and the Virgin Islands.

Jean Avnet Morse, Executive Director
Commission on Higher Education
3624 Market Street
Philadelphia, PA 19104-2680
Telephone: 215-662-5606
Fax: 215-662-5950
E-mail: info@msache.org
Web site: www.msache.org

New England Association of Schools and Colleges

Accredits institutions in Connecticut, Maine, Massachusetts, New Hampshire, Rhode Island, and Vermont.

Charles M. Cook, Director
Commission on Institutions of Higher Education
209 Burlington Road
Bedford, MA 01730-1433
Telephone: 781-271-0022
Fax: 781-271-0950
E-mail: ccook@neasc.org
Web site: www.neasc.org

North Central Association of Colleges and Schools

Accredits institutions in Arizona, Arkansas, Colorado, Illinois, Indiana, Iowa, Kansas, Michigan, Minnesota, Missouri, Nebraska, New Mexico, North Dakota, Ohio, Oklahoma, South Dakota, West Virginia, Wisconsin, and Wyoming.

Steve Crow, Executive Director
Commission on Institutions of Higher Education
30 North LaSalle Street, Suite 2400
Chicago, IL 60602-2504
Telephone: 312-263-0456

Fax: 312-263-7462
E-mail: scrow@hlcommission.org
Web site: www.ncahigherlearningcommission.org

Northwest Association of Schools and Colleges

Accredits institutions in Alaska, Idaho, Montana, Nevada, Oregon, Utah, and Washington.

Sandra E. Elman, Executive Director
Commission on Colleges
11130 Northeast 33rd Place, Suite 120
Bellevue, WA 98004
Telephone: 425-827-2005
Fax: 425-827-3395
E-mail: selman@cocnasc.org
Web site: www.cocnasc.org

Southern Association of Colleges and Schools

Accredits institutions in Alabama, Florida, Georgia, Kentucky, Louisiana, Mississippi, North Carolina, South Carolina, Tennessee, Texas, and Virginia.

James T. Rogers, Executive Director
Commission on Colleges
1866 Southern Lane
Decatur, GA 30033-4097
Telephone: 404-679-4500
Fax: 404-679-4558
E-mail: jrogers@sacscoc.org
Web site: www.sacs.org

Western Association of Schools and Colleges

Accredits institutions in California, Guam, and Hawaii.

Ralph A. Wolff, Executive Director
Accrediting Commission for Senior Colleges and Universities
985 Atlantic Avenue, Suite 100
Alameda, CA 94501
Telephone: 510-748-9001
Fax: 510-748-9797
E-mail: wascsr@wascsenior.org
Web site: www.wascweb.org

Institutional Accrediting Agencies—Other

Accrediting Council for Independent Colleges and Schools

Stephen D. Parker, Executive Director
750 First Street, NE, Suite 980
Washington, DC 20002-4241

Telephone: 202-336-6780
Fax: 202-842-2593
E-mail: info@acics.org
Web site: www.acics.org

Distance Education and Training Council

Michael P. Lambert, Executive Secretary
1601 Eighteenth Street, NW
Washington, DC 20009-2529
Telephone: 202-234-5100
Fax: 202-332-1386
E-mail: detc@detc.org
Web site: www.detc.org

Specialized Accrediting Agencies

Acupuncture

Dort S. Bigg, Executive Director
Accreditation Commission for Acupuncture and Oriental Medicine
1010 Wayne Avenue, Suite 1270
Silver Spring, MD 20910
Telephone: 301-608-9680
Fax: 301-608-9576
E-mail: ccaom@compuserve.com
Web site: www.ccaom.org

Art and Design

Samuel Hope, Executive Director
National Association of Schools of Art and Design
11250 Roger Bacon Drive, Suite 21
Reston, VA 20190
Telephone: 703-437-0700
Fax: 703-437-6312
E-mail: info@arts-accredit.org
Web site: www.arts-accredit.org

Chiropractic

Paul D. Walker, Executive Director
The Council on Chiropractic Education
8049 North 85th Way
Scottsdale, AZ 85258-4321
Telephone: 480-443-8877
Fax: 480-483-7333
E-mail: cce@cce-usa.org
Web site: www.cce-usa.org

Clinical Laboratory Science

Betty Craft, Chairman
National Accrediting Agency for Clinical Laboratory Sciences
8410 West Bryn Mawr Avenue, Suite 670
Chicago, IL 60631
Telephone: 312-714-8880
Fax: 312-714-8886
E-mail: naaclsinfo@naacls.org
Web site: www.naacls.org

Dance

Samuel Hope, Executive Director
National Association of Schools of Dance
11250 Roger Bacon Drive, Suite 21
Reston, VA 20190
Telephone: 703-437-0700
Fax: 703-437-6312
E-mail: info@arts-accredit.org
Web site: www.arts-accredit.org

Dentistry

Laura M. Neumann, D.D.S., M.P.H., Associate Executive Director, Education
American Dental Association
211 East Chicago Avenue, 18th Floor
Chicago, IL 60611
Telephone: 312-440-2500
Fax: 312-440-2800
E-mail: education@ada.org
Web site: www.ada.org

Education

Arthur Wise, President
National Council for Accreditation of Teacher Education
2010 Massachusetts Avenue, NW
Washington, DC 20036-1023
Telephone: 202-466-7496
Fax: 202-296-6620
E-mail: info@ncate.org
Web site: www.ncate.org

Engineering

George D. Peterson, Executive Director
Accreditation Board for Engineering and Technology, Inc.
111 Market Place, Suite 1050
Baltimore, MD 21202
Telephone: 410-347-7700

Fax: 410-625-2238
E-mail: accreditation@abet.org
Web site: www.abet.org

Environment

National Environmental Health Science and Protection
    Accreditation Council
720 South Colorado Boulevard, Suite 970-S
Denver, CO 80246-1925
Telephone: 303-756-9090
Fax: 303-691-9490
E-mail: staff@neha.org
Web site: www.neha.org/AccredCouncil.html

Forestry

Michele Harvey, Director, Science and Education
Committee on Education
Society of American Foresters
5400 Grosvenor Lane
Bethesda, MD 20814-2198
Telephone: 301-897-8720 Ext. 119
Fax: 301-897-3690
E-mail: harveym@safnet.org
Web site: www.safnet.org

Health Services Administration

Andrea Barone-Wodjouatt, Executive Director
Accrediting Commission on Education for Health Services
    Administration
730 11th Street, NW, Fourth Floor
Washington, DC 20001-4510
Telephone: 202-638-5131
Fax: 202-638-3429
E-mail: accredcom@aol.com
Web site: monkey.hmi.missouri.edu/acehsa

Interior Design

Kayem Dunn, Director
Foundation for Interior Design Education Research
60 Monroe Center, NW, Suite 300
Grand Rapids, MI 49503-2920
Telephone: 616-458-0400
Fax: 616-458-0460
E-mail: fider@fider.org
Web site: www.fider.org

Journalism and Mass Communications

Susanne Shaw, Executive Director
Accrediting Council on Education in Journalism and Mass
    Communications
School of Journalism
Stauffer-Flint Hall
University of Kansas
Lawrence, KS 66045
Telephone: 785-864-3986
Fax: 785-864-5225
E-mail: sshaw@kuhub.cc.ukans.edu
Web site: www.ukans.edu/P5acejmc

Landscape Architecture

Ronald C. Leighton, Accreditation Manager
Landscape Architectural Accreditation Board
American Society of Landscape Architects
636 Eye Street, NW
Washington, DC 20001-3736
Telephone: 202-898-2444
Fax: 202-898-1185
E-mail: rleighton@asla.org
Web site: www.asla.org/asla/

Law

Carl Monk, Executive Vice President and Executive Director
Accreditation Committee
Association of American Law Schools
1201 Connecticut Avenue, NW, Suite 800
Washington, DC 20036-2605
Telephone: 202-296-8851
Fax: 202-296-8869
E-mail: cmonk@aals.org
Web site: www.aals.org

John A. Sebert, Consultant on Legal Education
American Bar Association
750 North Lake Shore Drive
Chicago, IL 60611
Telephone: 312-988-6746
E-mail: legaled@abanet.org
Web site: www.abanet.org/legaled

Library

Mary Taylor, Assistant Director
Committee on Accreditation
American Library Association

50 East Huron Street
Chicago, IL 60611
Telephone: 800-545-2433 (toll-free)
Fax: 312-280-2433
E-mail: mtaylor@ala.org
Web site: www.ala.org/accreditation

Marriage and Family Therapy

Michael Bowers, Executive Director
American Association for Marriage and Family Therapy
1133 15th Street, NW, Suite 300
Washington, DC 20005-2710
Telephone: 202-452-0109
Fax: 202-232-2329
E-mail: COAMFTE@aamft.org
Web site: www.aamft.org

Medical Illustration

William C. Andrea, Chair
Accreditation Review Committee for the Medical Illustrator
St. Luke's Hospital
Instructional Resources
232 South Woods Mill Road
Chesterfield, MO 63017
Telephone: 314-205-6158
Fax: 314-205-6144
E-mail: andrwc@stlo.smhs.com
Web site: www.caahep.org/accreditation/mi/mi-accreditation.htm

Medicine

Liaison Committee on Medical Education
The LCME is administered in even-numbered years, beginning
    each July 1, by:
David P. Stevens, M.D., Secretary
Association of American Medical Colleges
2450 N Street, NW
Washington, DC 20037
Telephone: 202-828-0596
Fax: 202-828-1125
E-mail: dstevens@aamc.org
Web site: www.aamc.org
The LCME is administered in odd-numbered years, beginning each
    July 1, by:
Frank Simon, M.D., Secretary
American Medical Association
515 North State Street

Chicago, IL 60610
Telephone: 312-464-4657
Fax: 312-464-5830
E-mail: frank_simon@ama-assn.org
Web site: www.ama-assn.org

Music

Samuel Hope, Executive Director
National Association of Schools of Music
11250 Roger Bacon Drive, Suite 21
Reston, VA 20190
Telephone: 703-437-0700
Fax: 703-437-6312
E-mail: info@arts-accredit.org
Web site: www.arts-accredit.org

Naturopathic Medicine

Robert Lofft, Executive Director
Council on Naturopathic Medical Education
P.O. Box 11426
Eugene, OR 97440-3626
Telephone: 541-484-6028
E-mail: dir@cnme.org
Web site: www.cnme.org

Nurse Anesthesia

Betty J. Horton, Director of Accreditation
Council on Accreditation of Nurse Anesthesia Educational
    Programs
222 South Prospect Avenue, Suite 304
Park Ridge, IL 60068-4010
Telephone: 847-692-7050
Fax: 847-693-7137
E-mail: cwargin@compuserve.com
Web site: www.aana.com/coa

Nurse Midwifery

Betty Watts Carrington, Chair
Division of Accreditation
American College of Nurse-Midwives
818 Connecticut Avenue, NW, Suite 900
Washington, DC 20006
Telephone: 202-728-9877
Fax: 202-728-9897
E-mail: educatio@acnm.org
Web site: www.midwife.org/educ

Nursing

Geraldene Felton, Executive Director
National League for Nursing
61 Broadway, 33rd Floor
New York, NY 10006
Telephone: 800-669-1656 (toll-free)
Fax: 212-812-0393
E-mail: gfelton@nlnac.org
Web site: www.nln.org

Occupational Therapy

Doris Gordon, Director of Accreditation
American Occupational Therapy Association
4720 Montgomery Lane
P.O. Box 31220
Bethesda, MD 20824-1220
Telephone: 301-652-2682
Fax: 301-652-7711
E-mail: accred@aota.org
Web site: www.aota.org

Optometry

Joyce Urbeck, Administrative Director
Council on Optometric Education
American Optometric Association
243 North Lindbergh Boulevard
St. Louis, MO 63141
Telephone: 314-991-4100
Fax: 314-991-4101
E-mail: coe@theaoa.org
Web site: www.aoanet.org

Osteopathic Medicine

John B. Crosby, Executive Director
Bureau of Professional Education, Council on Predoctoral
   Education
American Osteopathic Association
142 East Ontario Street
Chicago, IL 60611
Telephone: 800-621-1773 (toll-free)
Fax: 312-202-8200
E-mail: ssweet@aoa-net.org
Web site: www.aoa-net.org

Pastoral Education

Reverend Teresa E. Snorton, Executive Director

Accreditation Commission
Association for Clinical Pastoral Education, Inc.
1549 Clairmont Road, Suite 103
Decatur, GA 30033-4611
Telephone: 404-320-1472
Fax: 404-320-0849
E-mail: teresa@acpe.edu
Web site: www.acpe.edu

Pharmacy

Peter H. Vlasses, Executive Director
American Council on Pharmaceutical Education
311 West Superior Street
Chicago, IL 60610
Telephone: 312-664-3575
Fax: 312-664-4652
E-mail: csinfo@acpe-accredit.org
Web site: www.acpe-accredit.org

Physical Therapy

Mary Jane Harris, Director
Department of Accreditation
American Physical Therapy Association
1111 North Fairfax Street
Alexandria, VA 22314-1488
Telephone: 800-999-2782 (toll-free) *or* 703-684-2782
Fax: 703-684-7343
E-mail: accreditation@apta.org
Web site: www.apta.org

Planning

Beatrice Clupper, Director
American Institute of Certified Planners/Association of Collegiate
   Schools of Planning
Merle Hay Tower, Suite 302
3800 Merle Hay Road
Des Moines, IA 50310
Telephone: 515-252-0729
Fax: 515-252-7404
E-mail: fi_pab@netins.net
Web site: netins.net/web/pab_fi66

Podiatric Medicine

Alan R. Tinkleman, Director
Council on Podiatric Medical Education
American Podiatric Medical Association

9312 Old Georgetown Road
Bethesda, MD 20814-1698
Telephone: 301-571-9200
Fax: 301-530-2752
E-mail: sbsaylor@apma.org
Web site: www.apm.org/cpme

Psychology and Counseling

Susan F. Zlotlow, Director
Committee on Accreditation
American Psychological Association
750 First Street, NE
Washington, DC 20002-4242
Telephone: 202-336-5979
Fax: 202-336-5978
E-mail: apaaccred@apa.org
Web site: www.apa.org/ed/accred.html
Carol L. Bobby, Executive Director
Council for Accreditation of Counseling and Related Educational
    Programs
American Counseling Association
5999 Stevenson Avenue, Fourth Floor
Alexandria, VA 22304
Telephone: 800-347-6647 Ext. 301 (toll-free)
Fax: 703-823-1581
E-mail: cacrep@aol.com
Web site: www.counseling.org/CACREP

Public Affairs and Administration

Michael A. Brintnall, Executive Director
Commission on Peer Review and Accreditation
National Association of Schools of Public Affairs and
    Administration
1120 G Street, NW, Suite 730
Washington, DC 20005
Telephone: 202-628-8965
Fax: 202-626-4978
E-mail: naspaa@naspaa.org
Web site: www.naspaa.org

Public Health

Patricia Evans, Executive Director
Council on Education for Public Health
800 I Street, NW, Suite 202
Washington, DC 20001-3710
Telephone: 202-789-1050

Fax: 202-789-1895
E-mail: patevans@ceph.org
Web site: www.ceph.org

Rabbinical and Talmudic Education

Bernard Fryshman, Executive Vice President
Association of Advanced Rabbinical and Talmudic Schools
175 Fifth Avenue, Suite 711
New York, NY 10010
Telephone: 212-477-0950
Fax: 212-533-5335

Rehabilitation Education

Jeanne Patterson, Executive Director
Council on Rehabilitation Education
Commission on Standards and Accreditation
1835 Rohlwing Road, Suite E
Rolling Meadows, IL 60008
Telephone: 847-394-1785
Fax: 847-394-2108
E-mail: patters@polaris.net
Web site: www.core-rehab.org

Social Work

Nancy Randolph, Director
Council on Social Work Education
1725 Duke Street, Suite 500
Alexandria, VA 22314
Telephone: 703-683-8080
Fax: 703-683-8099
E-mail: accred@cswe.org
Web site: www.cswe.org

Speech-Language Pathology and Audiology

Sharon Goldsmith, Director
American Speech-Language-Hearing Association
10801 Rockville Pike
Rockville, MD 20852
Telephone: 301-897-5700
Fax: 301-571-0457
E-mail: accreditation@asha.org
Web site: www.asha.org

Theater

Samuel Hope, Executive Director
National Association of Schools of Theatre

11250 Roger Bacon Drive, Suite 21
Reston, VA 20190
Telephone: 703-437-0700
Fax: 703-437-6312
E-mail: info@arts-accredit.org
Web site: www.arts-accredit.org

Theology

Daniel O. Aleshire, Executive Director
Association of Theological Schools in the United States and Canada
10 Summit Park Drive
Pittsburgh, PA 15275-1103
Telephone: 412-788-6505
Fax: 412-788-6510
E-mail: ats@ats.edu
Web site: www.ats.edu

Veterinary Medicine

Donald G. Simmons, Director of Education and Research Division
American Veterinary Medical Association
1931 North Meacham Road, Suite 100
Schaumburg, IL 60173
Telephone: 847-925-8070
Fax: 847-925-1329
E-mail: dsimmons@avma.org
Web site: www.avma.org

Accreditation in Canada

To get general information about accreditation in Canada, visit the Web site of the Council of Ministers of Education. Their Web site also has contact information and links to the provincial departments of education.

Council of Ministers of Education, Canada
95 St. Clair Avenue West, Suite 1106
Toronto, Ontario
Canada M4V 1N6
Telephone: 416-962-8100
Fax: 416-962-2800
E-mail: cmec@cmec.ca
Web site: www.cmec.ca

Other Resources for Evaluating Programs

Bear, Mariah P., John Bear, and John B. Bear. *Bear's Guide to Earning Degrees Nontraditionally, 13th ed. Ten Speed Press, 1999.*

Quality on the Line: Benchmarks for Success in Internet-Based Distance Education. Washington, DC: The Institute for Higher Education Policy, March 2000. Available at www.ihep.com/qualityonline.pdf

Chapter 6: Taking Standardized Admissions Tests

SATs

For information about the SATs, contact the College Board:

SAT Program
The College Board
P.O. Box 6202
Princeton, NJ 08541-6202
Telephone: 609-771-7600
E-mail: sat@info.collegeboard.org
Web site: www.collegeboard.org

The College Board offers free preparation advice and a practice test in *Taking the SAT I: Reasoning Test* and preparation suggestions in *Taking the SAT II: Subject Area Test.* Call them to get a copy. The Web site also offers other test-preparation materials, including books, videos, and software, for a charge. Order at www.collegeboard.org or call 609-771-7243:

10 Real SATs. 600 pp. 1997.

Real SAT II: Subject Tests. 840 pp. 1998.

Look inside the SAT I. Video, 30 minutes, 1994.

One-on-One with the SAT. Software, 1995.

Other test-preparation resources:

Crystal, Michael R. *SAT Math Flash.* Princeton, NJ: Peterson's, 1997.

SAT Success 2001. Princeton, NJ: Peterson's, 2000.

ACT Assessment

ACT Registration
P.O. Box 414
Iowa City, IA 52243-0414
Telephone: 319-337-1270
Web site: www.act.org/aap

The Web site offers test-preparation strategies, sample questions, and information about other ACT resources.

Bender, Elaine, et al. *ACT Success (with CD).* Princeton, NJ: Peterson's, 2000.

GREs

For information about the GREs, contact the Educational Testing Service:

> GRE-ETS
> PO Box 6000
> Princeton, NJ 08541-6000
> Telephone: (609) 771-7670
> E-mail: gre-info@ets.org
> Web site (GRE Online): www.gre.org

The Web site offers a lot of material that can be downloaded: information bulletins, practice tests, descriptions of the subject area tests, and preparation software. Order from ETS at www.gre.org:

> *GRE Big Book*
>
> GRE Powerprep Software. Includes test preparation for both the General Test and the Writing Assessment.
>
> *GRE Practicing to Take the General Test*
>
> Practice Books for Subject Area Tests

Other resources:

> *GRE CAT Success.* A workbook and CD that provide strategies and practice for the GRE. Princeton, NJ: Peterson's, 2000.
> Practice Books for Subject Area Tests.

MAT

The Psychological Corporation
555 Academic Court
San Antonio, TX 78204
Telephone: (800) 622-3231 (toll-free)
Web site: www.tpcweb.com/mat

Bader, William, and Daniel S. Burt. *Master the MAT.* Arco, 2000.

GMAT

GMAT
Distribution and Receiving Center
225 Phillips Boulevard
Ewing, NJ 08628-7435
Telephone: 609-771-7330
E-mail: gmat@ets.org
Web site (MBA Explorer): www.gmac.com

GMAT Success. Princeton, NJ: Peterson's, 2000.

TOEFL and TSE

Information on both the TOEFL and the TSE can be obtained from the Educational Testing Service:

TOEFL
PO Box 6151
Princeton, NJ 08541-6151
Telephone: 609-771-7100
E-mail: toefl@ets.org
Web site: toefl.org

Rogers, Bruce. *TOEFL Practice Tests.* Princeton, NJ: Peterson's, 2000. Can be purchased with audiocassettes to prepare for the listening section.

—*TOEFL Success.* Princeton, NJ: Peterson's, 2000.

Chapter 7: Applying for Admission to Degree Programs

Davidson, Wilma, and Susan McCloskey. *Writing a Winning College Application Essay.* Princeton, NJ: Peterson's, 2000.

Hayden, Thoms C. *Insider's Guide to College Admissions.* Princeton, NJ: Peterson's, 2000.

Stelzer, Richard J. *How to Write a Winning Personal Statement for Graduate and Professional School, 3d ed.* Princeton, NJ: Peterson's, 1997. Lots of suggestions, both from the author and admissions representatives of graduate and professional schools, along with many sample essays.

Chapter 8: Paying for Your Education

General Information

Financial Aid Information Page (www.finaid.org). The best place to start an Internet search for financial aid information.

McWade, Patricia. *Financing Graduate School.* Princeton, NJ: Peterson's, 1996. The best, most detailed treatment of financial aid for graduate students, written by the dean of student financial services at Georgetown University.

National Association of Student Financial Aid Administrators (www.nasfaa.org). Lots of essays explain various aspects of financial aid, including educational tax credits.

Turlington, Shannon R. *The Unofficial Guide to Financing a College Education.* Arco, 1999.

State Residency

Todd, Daryl F., Jr. *How to Cut Tuition: The Complete Guide to In-State Tuition*. Linwood, NJ: Atlantic Educational Publishing, 1997.

Federal Aid

Federal Student Aid Information Center
P.O. Box 84
Washington, DC 20044-0084
Telephone: 800-4-FED-AID (toll-free) (general information, assistance, and publications)
Web sites:
General information and home page: www.ed.gov/studentaid

For a copy of *2000–2001 Financial Aid: The Student Guide:* www.ed.gov/prog_info/SFA/StudentGuide.
For the FAFSA, go to FAFSA Online: www.fafsa.ed.gov.
For more on the Distance Education Demonstration Program: www.ed.gov/offices/OPE/PPI/DistEd/proginfo.html

State Agencies of Higher Education

Alabama: 334-242-2274
Alaska: 907-465-6741
Arizona: 602-229-2591
Arkansas: 800-547-8839 (toll-free)
California: 916-526-7590
Colorado: 303-866-2723
Connecticut: 860-947-1855
Delaware: 800-292-7935 (toll-free)
District of Columbia: 202-698-2400
Florida: 888-827-2004 (toll-free)
Georgia: 770-724-9030 or 404-656-5969
Hawaii: 808-956-8213
Idaho: 208-334-2270
Illinois: 800-899-4722 (toll-free)
Indiana: 317-232-2350
Iowa: 515-242-3344
Kansas: 785-296-3517
Kentucky: 800-928-8926 (toll-free)
Louisiana: 800-259-5626 (toll-free)
Maine: 800-228-3734 (toll-free)
Maryland: 410-260-4565
Massachusetts: 617-727-9420
Michigan: 877-323-2287 (toll-free)
Minnesota: 800-657-3866 (toll-free)

Mississippi: 601-432-6997
Missouri: 800-473-6757 (toll-free)
Montana: 800-537-7508 (toll-free)
Nebraska: 402-471-2847
Nevada: 775-687-9228
New Hampshire: 603-271-2555
New Jersey: 800-792-8670 (toll-free)
New Mexico: 800-279-9777 (toll-free)
New York: 800-642-6234 (toll-free)
North Carolina: 800-600-3453 (toll-free)
North Dakota: 701-328-4114
Ohio: 888-833-1133 (toll-free)
Oklahoma: 800-858-1840 (toll-free)
Oregon: 800-452-8807 (toll-free)
Pennsylvania: 800-692-7392 or 7435(toll-free)
Rhode Island: 800-922-9855 (toll-free)
South Carolina: 803-737-2260
South Dakota: 605-773-3134
Tennessee: 800-342-1663 (toll-free)
Texas: 800-242-3062 (toll-free)
Utah: 800-418-8757 (toll-free)
Vermont: 800-642-3177 (toll-free)
Virginia: 804-786-1690
Washington: 360-753-7850
West Virginia: 888-825-5707 (toll-free)
Wisconsin: 608-267-2206
Wyoming: 307-777-7763
Guam: 671-475-0457
Northern Mariannas: 670-234-6128
Puerto Rico: 787-724-7100
Republic of Palau: 680-488-2471
Virgin Islands: 340-774-4546

CSS Financial Aid Profile

Contact the College Scholarship Service at www.collegeboard.org
   or 305-829-9793.

Grants, Fellowships, and Scholarships

AJR Newslink (www.newslink.org). Awards, grants, and scholarships
   for journalism students.

Annual Register of Grant Support: A Directory of Funding Sources.
   Wilmette, IL.: National Register Publishing Company.

College Money Handbook 2001. Princeton, NJ: Peterson's, 2000.

CollegeQuest (www.CollegeQuest.com). Online searchable database of scholarships and fellowships.

Corporate Foundation Profiles. New York: Foundation Center, 1999 (fdncenter.org or 212-620-4230).

FastWeb (fastweb.com). Online searchable database of scholarships and fellowships.

Peterson's Grants for Graduate and Postdoctoral Study, 5th ed. Compiled by the University of Massachusetts, Amherst. Princeton, NJ: Peterson's, 1998. More than 1,400 fellowships and other awards, indexed by field of study as well as special characteristics of the recipients (e.g., ethnic minority groups).

Scholarships and Loans for Adult Students. Princeton, NJ: Peterson's, 2000.

Scholarships, Grants, & Prizes 2001. Princeton, NJ: Peterson's, 2000.

Cooperative Education

Re, Joseph M. *Earn and Learn.* Octameron Associates, 1997.

Credit Reporting Agencies

It's a good idea to check your credit rating before you apply for any loans. Call first to find out if there is a fee.

Experian
PO Box 9530
Allen, TX 75013
Telephone: 888-397-3742 (toll-free)

Equifax
PO Box 105873
Atlanta, GA 30348
Telephone: 800-685-1111 (toll-free)

CSC Credit Services
Consumer Assistance Center
PO Box 674402
Houston, TX 77267-4402
Telephone: 800-759-5979 (toll-free)

Trans Union Corporation
PO Box 390
Springfield, PA 19064-0390
Telephone: 800-888-4213 (toll-free)

Tax Issues

Educational Expenses, IRS Publication 508.

Tax Benefits for Higher Education. IRS Publication 970.

To get a copy of these publications, visit the Internal Revenue Service Web site at www.irs.ustreas.gov/prod/forms_pubs/pubs or call 800-829-3676 (toll-free).

Women, Minority Students, Disabled Students, and Veterans

Bruce-Young, Doris M., and William C. Young. *Higher Education Money Book for Women and Minorities.* Young Enterprises International, 1997.

Minority and Women's Complete Scholarship Book; plus Scholarships for Religious Affiliations and People with Disabilities. Sourcebooks, 1998.

Olson, Elizabeth A. *Dollars for College (Women).* Garrett Park Press, 1995.

Saludos Web Education Center (www.saludos.com). Internships and scholarships targeted to Hispanic Americans as well as those not considering race or ethnicity.

Schlachter, Gail Ann, and R. David Weber. *Financial Aid for African Americans.* Reference Service Press, 1997.

Schlachter, Gail Ann, and R. David Weber. *Financial Aid for the Disabled and Their Families.* Reference Service Press, 1998.

Schlachter, Gail Ann, and R. David Weber. *Financial Aid for Veterans, Military Personnel, and Their Dependents.* Reference Service Press, 1996.

Schlachter, Gail Ann. *Directory of Financial Aid for Women.* Reference Service Press, 1997.

International Students

Funding for U.S. Study—A Guide for International Students and Professionals and *Financial Resources for International Study.* New York: Institute of International Education (www.iiebooks.org).

Chapter 9: Succeeding as a Distance Learner

Bruno, Frank J. *Going Back to School: College Survival Strategies for Adult Students.* New York, Arco, 1998.

accreditation—In the United States, the process by which private, nongovernmental educational agencies with regional or national scope certify that colleges and universities provide educational programs at basic levels of quality

ACT Assessment—a standardized undergraduate admissions test that is based on the typical high school curriculum

associate's degree—a degree awarded upon the successful completion of a prebaccalaureate level program, usually consisting of two years of full-time study at the college level

asynchronous—not simultaneous or concurrent; for example, discussion groups in online courses are asynchronous because students can log on and post messages at any time

audioconferencing—electronic meeting in which participants in remote locations can communicate with one another using telephones or speakerphones

bachelor's degree—a degree awarded upon the successful completion of about four years of full-time college-level study

bandwidth—the width of frequencies required to transmit a communications signal without too much distortion. Video, animation, and sound require more bandwidth than text.

broadband—a high-speed, high-capacity transmission channel carried on coaxial or fiber-optic cable; it has a higher *bandwidth* than telephone lines and so can transmit more data more quickly than telephone lines

broadcast radio and television—radio and television programs sent out over the airwaves; one of the earliest distance learning technologies that is still used

browser—a computer program used to view, download, upload, or otherwise access documents (sites) on the World Wide Web

bulletin board—a site on the Internet where people can post messages

cable television—television programming transmitted over optical fiber, coaxial, or twisted pair (telephone) cables

CD-ROM—Compact disc, read-only memory; an optical storage technology that allows you to store and play back data

certificate—an educational credential awarded upon completion of a structured curriculum, typically including several courses but lasting for a period of less time than that required for a degree

certification—the awarding of a credential, usually by a professional or industry group, usually after a course of study and the passing of an exam

chat room—a site on the Internet in which people can communicate synchronously by typing messages to one another

CLEP—the College Level Examination Program, administered by the College Board, that tests students' subject knowledge in order to award college-level credit for noncollegiate learning

common application form—a standardized basic admissions application form, available on line, that is used by many colleges

consortium—a group of colleges and universities that pool resources to enable students to take courses as needed from all participating institutions

Game Plan for Distance Learning

continuing education unit—10 contact hours of participation in an organized continuing education program; a nationwide, standardized measure of continuing education courses

correspondence course—individual or self-guided study by mail from a college or university for which credit is typically granted through written assignments and proctored examinations; also referred to as *independent study*

correspondence school—a school whose primary means of delivering instruction is via *correspondence courses*

cost of attendance—the total cost, including tuition, fees, living expenses, books, supplies, and miscellaneous expenses, of attending a particular school for an academic year

CSS Profile—the College Scholarship Service's Financial Aid Profile form, a standardized financial aid application form used by many colleges and universities

DANTES Subject Standardized Tests—a series of equivalency examinations used primarily by the U.S. Department of Defense but available to civilians as well

distance learning—the delivery of educational programs to students who are off site; also called *distance education*

doctoral degree—the highest degree awarded upon demonstrated mastery of a subject, including the ability to do scholarly research

DVD—digital video disc; an optical storage technology that allows you to store and retrieve audio and video data

e-learning—distance learning via the Internet

electronic bulletin board—an "area" of the Internet in which people can post messages

e-mail—text or other messages sent over the Internet; also called *electronic mail*

enrollment status—whether a student is enrolled full-time, three-quarter time, half-time, or less than half-time in a degree or certificate program

equivalency examination—an examination similar to the final exam of a college-level course; if you pass, you may be awarded college-level credit; for example, the CLEP and DANTES exams

Expected Family Contribution (EFC)—The amount a student and his or her family are expected to contribute to the cost of the student's education per academic year

FAFSA—the Free Application for Federal Student Aid, a form needed to apply for federal aid programs

fax machine—a telecopying device that transmits written or graphic material over telephone lines to produce a hard copy at a remote location; also called a *facsimile machine*

Federal Supplemental Educational Opportunity Grant (FSEOG)—a federal grant awarded to students that demonstrate the greatest financial need

fellowship—a gift, to be used for a student's education, that does not have to be repaid; also called a *grant* or *scholarship*

financial need—the amount of money a student needs to be given or loaned, or earn through work-study, in order to attend school for one year. It is calculated by subtracting Estimated Family Contribution from cost of attendance.

first-professional degree—a degree awarded upon the successful completion of a program of study for which a bachelor's degree is normally the prerequisite and that prepares a student for a specific profession

GMAT—the Graduate Management Admissions Test, a standardized test used by many graduate programs in business

graduate degree—a degree awarded upon the successful completion of a program of study at the postbaccalaureate level; usually a master's or doctoral degree

grant—a gift, to be used for a student's education, that does not have to be repaid; also called a *scholarship* or *fellowship*

GRE General Test—the Graduate Record Examinations General Test, which tests verbal, quantitative and analytical skills; usually taken by prospective graduate students

GRE Subject Area Tests—examinations that assess knowledge usually acquired in college-level courses

instructional design—the way course content is organized for the learner; it varies from one distance technology to another

Internet—the global computer "network of networks" that allows for the transmission of words, images, and sound to anyone with an Internet connection; it has become one of the major instructional delivery systems for distance learning

Internet service provider (ISP)—a company such as AOL or Earthlink that serves as a gateway to the Internet; by subscribing to its service, an individual can connect to the Internet

life experience—a basis for earning college credit, usually demonstrated by means of a portfolio

LSAT—the Law School Admissions Test, taken by law school applicants

master's degree—a degree awarded upon the successful completion of a program of study beyond the baccalaureate level, typically requires one or two years of full-time study

MAT—the Miller Analogies Test, a standardized admissions test used by some graduate programs

MCAT—the Medical College Admissions Test, taken by medical school applicants

merit-based aid—funding awarded on the basis of academic merit, regardless of financial need

modem—MOdulator DEModulator; a device that allows a computer to connect with other computers (and therefore the Internet) over telephone lines. The faster the modem speed, the faster data is transmitted.

need-based aid—financial aid awarded on the basis of financial need; it may take the form of grants, loans, or work-study

online course—a course offered primarily over the Internet

online learning—distance learning via the Internet; sometimes called *e-learning*

Pell Grant—a federal grant that is awarded to students on the basis of financial need

Perkins Loan—a loan offered by the federal government to students with exceptional financial need

PowerPoint—a software program that enables the user to prepare slides with text, graphics, and sound; often used by instructors in their class presentations

Excelsior College Examinations—a series of equivalency examinations administered by Excelsior College; formerly the Regents College Examinations

SAT I—the Scholastic Aptitude Test I, a standardized undergraduate admissions test

SAT II—subject area tests that assess high school level knowledge; used by some schools for undergraduate admissions

satellite television—programming beamed to an orbiting satellite, then retrieved by one or more ground-based satellite dishes

scholarship—a gift, to be used for a student's education, that does not have to be repaid; also called a *grant* or *fellowship*

Stafford Loan—a loan, either subsidized or unsubsidized, offered by the federal government

streaming video—high *bandwidth* video data transmission

synchronous—occurring simultaneously, in real time

Title IV funds—federal money disbursed to eligible students through eligible, accredited institutions of higher learning or directly from the government

TOEFL—the Test of English as a Foreign Language, taken by students who are not native speakers of English

two-way interactive video—two-way communication of video and audio signals so that people in remote locations can see and hear one another

videoconferencing—one-way video and two-way audio transmission, or two-way video transmission conducted via satellite; instructors and students can communicate among remote locations

videotaped lecture—recording of an on-campus lecture or class session; usually mailed to distance learners enrolled in the course

virtual university—a college or university that offers most or all of its instruction exclusively via technology and usually for a profit

whiteboard—a program that allows multiple users at their own computers to draw and write comments on the same document

work-study award—an amount a student earns through part-time work as part of the federal work-study program